The Fingerhut Guide

Santa Barbara, California
Oxford, England

The Fingerhut Guide

Sources in American History

Eugene R. Fingerhut

Library of Congress Catalog Card Number 72-95266
ISBN Paperbound Edition 0-87436-117-6

American Bibliographical Center—Clio Press, Inc.
2040 Alameda Padre Serra
Santa Barbara, California

European Bibliographical Center—Clio Press
30 Cornmarket Street
Oxford OX1 3EY, England

Designed by Barbara Monahan
Composed by Camera-Ready Composition
Printed and bound by Consolidated Printers, Inc.
in the United States of America

MARILYN—friend, wife, inamorata

CONTENTS

INTRODUCTION

This guide is meant for persons researching topics in American history. It fills a void which has long vexed the lay researcher, the undergraduate student, and the first-year graduate student who must frequently seek a researchable topic, find necessary information, arrange and digest the data, and present the information within a limited period. They must cull material from nearby libraries and repositories. They are faced with obstacles which inhibit full investigation of a subject. Proper use of this guide will hopefully shorten the time spent in searching for information and increase the number of sources which can be investigated.

This can be accomplished by fully utilizing the bibliographies cited. It is obviously a waste of time and effort for the researcher to create a full bibliography on a subject when one already exists. This guide is an aid to finding bibliographies on specific topics. If the bounds of the subject to be researched are already delineated, the user will probably prefer to seek immediate aid in Part I of this guide, where he will find American history divided into topics. See the table of contents for the specific topics covered. This guide will be most efficiently used to research subjects on which a bibliography has already been prepared. Parts of several bibliographies and several other types of research sources should be consulted to find written material on subjects not covered by published bibliographies.

Part I of this guide is selective, including material published only between 1942 and 1972. The revised edition of Henry Putney Beers' *Bibliographies in American History: Guide to Materials for Research* was published in 1942 and there is no need to duplicate material in Beers' overwhelming compilation. Nor is this guide meant to bring Beers' work up to date. Many types of sources in Beers' *Bibliographies* are omitted here because they are unavailable to the researcher for whom this guide is intended. Privately printed pamphlets and books or materials of limited editions are also not included. This guide considers bibliographies accessible in most research, university, and central metropolitan reference libraries.

The reason for the omission of rare reference guides is obvious. For example, a limited edition bibliography published at the University of Seattle is of little value to an undergraduate researcher in Atlanta, Georgia. A doctoral candidate at the University of Chicago may have time to employ interlibrary loan facilities to obtain a rare University of Virginia reference publication—he has years to spend on his dissertation. But a seminar student at the same institution or a researcher in business must present his findings within less time. The availability of sources was a crucial consideration in determining whether a particular bibliography was to be included in Part I of this guide.

Part I contains only bibliographic volumes. Bibliographic articles have been omitted because indexes and abstracts which make periodic literature easily accessible are legion. Part II, "Indexes & Abstracts," is devoted to the use of research sources that yield valuable periodical material, if it is needed. Guides to manuscripts are not included since they can be found in the sources mentioned in Part II, "Basic Reference Guides to Social Sciences & to History." Guides to manuscript collections are omitted because time and money limitations usually put remote manuscript collections beyond the reach of most researchers. Researchers should consult local reference librarians to exploit manuscript collections available for use.

Part II contains general references to aid in finding sources and material not included in Part I. It is a necessary tool to be used in developing leads to information in Part I, or to find other sources not mentioned previously. No research project should be completed until the basic references, subject indexes, and other sources listed in Part II are exploited. The sources suggested in Part II will lead the researcher to references on almost every topic of human knowledge.

Part I of the guide offers the student access to bibliographic volumes in American history which may be found in most American libraries. Part II references major general bibliographies, catalogs, indexes, guides, and abstracts which will expand the usable amount of information for a variety of research topics.

This guide was compiled with the aid of many persons. The reference librarians of the John F. Kennedy Library at California State University, Los Angeles, were particularly helpful. Martha Hackman read the manuscript and offered the fruits of her bibliographic expertise, and Richard Brome located many government publications. Of the many students who have contributed bits, the inspired curiosity and diligence of Jeannine Caruso, Donald Delano, and Barry Helfand were outstanding. Richard Dean Burns, my colleague, appreciated the need for this guide and offered much of the inspiration needed to maintain my efforts. Lloyd Garrison, of ABC-Clio, and his staff of editors and advisors are responsible for much of the merit of this guide. To my copy editor, proof reader, indexer, gadfly, and wife—Marilyn—I can express only my deepest thanks, and my respect for her ability to master the rules of punctuation and spelling.

I alone am responsible for sources of information included and omitted and for the organization of this guide. As I welcome compliments, I also accept responsibility for deficiencies and errors.

Part I

Bibliographies

The references cited in Part I are listed under topical and geographic subheadings within each section. Fully cited (i.e., cross-referenced entries) are consecutively numbered. Consult the numbered entries to find publisher, place, and date of publication of the work cited.

1 / PERSONAL ACCOUNTS

Collective Autobiography & Biography

Includes bibliographies which consider personal accounts of several people who have a common experience (e.g., businessmen, musicians, judges). Also includes collections of autobiographies and diaries. See also: PERSONAL ACCOUNTS: Individual Autobiography & Biography; INTELLECTUAL & CULTURAL LIFE: Exploration & Travel; subject sections for prominent men in specific endeavors (e.g., INTELLECTUAL & CULTURAL LIFE: Literature, Poetry, & Philosophy; SOCIAL LIFE: Religion).

[1] Bailey, Rosalie Fellows. *Guide to Genealogical and Biographical Sources for New York City (Manhattan) 1783-1898.* New York: n.p., 1954. 96 pp. Organized by topic. Index. Most items annotated.

Blanck. *American Literature.* (See 438)

Clark. *Literature: Poe Through Garland.* (See 439)

Dahl and Bolden. *The American Judge.* (See 329)

[2] Dargan, Marion. *Guide to American Biography.* 2 vols. Albuquerque: University of New Mexico, 1949-1952. Organized chronologically by generations. Index. Most items annotated.

[3] Filby, P. William. *American & British Genealogy & Heraldry; a Selected List of Books.* Chicago: American Library Association, 1970. 184 pp. Organized by topic. Index. Annotated.

[4] Freitag, Ruth S. *Presidential Inaugurations: a Selected List of References.* 3d ed. Washington, D.C.: General Reference and Bibliography

Division, Library of Congress, 1969. 230 pp. Organized chronologically. Index. Not annotated.

Gerstenberger and Hendrick. *Criticism on Novels.* (See 445)

Harvard University. *Studies in Enterprise.* (See 57)

Havlice. *Author Bibliographies.* (See 450)

Holman. *American Novel.* (See 452)

Jones and Ripley. *Parties in Congress.* (See 300)

[5] Kaplan, Louis. *A Bibliography of American Autobiographies [1676-1900].* Madison: University of Wisconsin, 1961. 372 pp. Organized alphabetically by author. Index. Most items annotated.

Kennington. *Jazz.* (See 493)

Lawrenz. *Negro Music.* (See 494)

[6] Lillard, Richard Gordon. *American Life in Autobiography, a Descriptive Guide.* Stanford: Stanford University, 1956. 140 pp. Organized by topic. Index. Annotated.

[7] Matthews, William, and Pearce, Roy. *American Diaries; an Annotated Bibliography of American Diaries Written Prior to the Year 1861.* Berkeley: University of California, 1945. 383 pp. Organized by date of publication. Index. Annotated.

Merriam and Benford. *Jazz.* (See 498)

New York Historical Society. *Artists.* (See 433)

[8] Nicholson, Margaret E. *People in Books; a Selective Guide to Biographical Literature Arranged by Vocations and other Fields of Reader Interest.* New York: Wilson, 1969. 498 pp. Organized by topic. Index. Not annotated.

[9] Sable, Martin H. *A Bio-Bibliography of the Kennedy Family.* Metuchen, N.J.: Scarecrow, 1969. 330 pp. Organized by topic. Index. Not annotated.

[10] Slocum, Robert B. *Biographical Dictionaries and Related Works; an International Bibliography of Collective Biographies.* Detroit: Gale Research, 1967. 1,056 pp. Organized by nation. Index. Not annotated.

Smith. *Personal Names.* (See 526)

Tompkins. *Supreme Court.* (See 337)

[11] U.S. Library of Congress. General Reference and Bibliography Division. *Biographical Sources for the United States.* Washington, D.C.: G.P.O., 1961. 58 pp. Organized by topic. Index. Annotated.

U.S. Library of Congress. General Reference and Bibliography Division. *Poets.* (See 462)

[12] U.S. Library of Congress. General Reference and Bibliography Division. *Presidents of the United States, 1789-1962; Selected List of References.* Washington, D.C.: G.P.O., 1962. 159 pp. Organized by topic. Index. Minority of items annotated.

Individual Autobiography & Biography

Includes bibliographies which consider personal accounts of an individual person (e.g., politicians, inventors, colorful personalities). Included here are persons *not* known primarily as writers. Citations are in alphabetical order by subject. See also: PERSONAL ACCOUNTS: Collective Autobiography & Biography; and subject sections for prominent men in specific endeavors (e.g., INTELLECTUAL & CULTURAL LIFE: Literature, Poetry, & Philosophy; SOCIAL LIFE: Religion).

[13] Dykes, Jefferson Chenworth. *Billy the Kid.* Albuquerque: University of New Mexico, 1952. 186 pp. Organized by date of publication. Index. Annotated.

[14] U.S. Library of Congress. General Reference and Bibliography Division. *Christopher Columbus; a Selected List of Books and Articles by American Authors or Published in America, 1892-1950.* Washington, D.C.: G.P.O., 1950. 37 pp. Organized alphabetically by author. No index. Annotated.

Johnson and Reeve. *Daniel De Leon.* (See 467)

Thomas. *John Dewey.* (See 468)

[15] Crown, James Tracy. *The Kennedy Literature: a Bibliographical Essay on John F. Kennedy.* New York: New York University, 1968. 181 pp. Organized by topic. Index. Well annotated.

[16] U.S. Library of Congress. General Reference and Bibliography Division. *John F. Kennedy, 1917-1963; a Chronological List of References.* Washington, D.C.: G.P.O., 1964. 68 pp. Organized by date of publication. Index. Not annotated.

Fishwick and Hollis. *R.E. Lee.* (See 239)

[17] Angle, Paul M. *A Shelf of Lincoln Books.* New Brunswick, N.J.: Rutgers University, 1946. 142 pp. Organized by type of publication. Index. Annotated.

[18] Searcher, Victor. *Lincoln Today; an Introduction to Modern Lincolniana.* New York: Thomas Yoseloff, 1969. 342 pp. Organized by type of publication. Index. Annotated.

[19] Servies, James Albert. *A Bibliography of John Marshall.* Washington, D.C.: U.S. Commission for the Celebration of the 200th Anniversary of the Birth of John Marshall, 1956. 182 pp. Organized by date of publication and alphabetically by author. Index. Annotated.

Setaro. *Roscoe Pound.* (See 334)

[20] The Franklin D. Roosevelt Library, Hyde Park, New York. *Calendar of the Speeches and other Public Statements of Franklin D. Roosevelt, 1910-1920.* Hyde Park, N.Y.: Author, 1952. 160 pp. Organized chronologically by statement. Index. Annotated.

[21] Halter, Ernest J. *Collecting First Editions of Franklin Roosevelt; Contributions to an FDR Bibliography.* Chicago: privately printed, 1949. 194 pp. Organized alphabetically by author. No index. Annotated.

Stewart. *Era of Franklin D. Roosevelt.* (See 576)

[22] Turnbull, Laura Shearer. *Woodrow Wilson, a Selected Bibliography of His Published Writings, Addresses and Public Papers.* Princeton: Princeton University, 1948. 173 pp. Organized by type of publication. Index. Not annotated.

[23] Renstrom, Arthur George. *Wilbur and Orville Wright; a Bibliography Commemorating the Hundredth Anniversary of the Birth of Wilbur Wright, April 16, 1967.* Washington, D.C.: Library of Congress, 1968. 187 pp. Organized by topic. Index. Minority of items annotated.

2 / FOREIGN AFFAIRS

General & Miscellaneous

Includes bibliographies which consider United States international relations not limited by geographic region, and general foreign policy covering several regions or topics. Also included are world affairs and national bibliographies useful for studying United States relations with other countries. See also: PERSONAL ACCOUNTS: Collective and Individual Autobiography & Biography; MILITARY: General & Miscellaneous, and Wars; POLITICS: Political Science & Miscellaneous.

American University. *Counterinsurgency.* (See 225)

[24] American University. Special Operations Research Office. *A Psychological Operations Bibliography.* Washington, D.C.: Author, 1960. 174 pp. Supplements to 1965. Organized alphabetically by author. No index. Annotated.

American University. *Unconventional Warfare.* (See 226)

Beers. *The French and British in the Old Northwest.* (See 132)

[25] Boehm, Eric H. *Bibliographies on International Relations and World Affairs; an Annotated Directory.* Santa Barbara, Calif.: ABC-Clio, 1965. 33 pp. Organized alphabetically by title. No index. Annotated.

[26] Brown, J. Cudd, and Rieg, Michael B. *Administration of United States Foreign Affairs.* University Park: Pennsylvania State University, 1968. 126 pp. Organized by topic. No index. Not annotated.

Crabbs and Holmquist. *Higher Education and World Affairs.* (See 552)

[27] Davis, Vincent, and Gilbert, Arthur N. *Basic Courses in International Relations; an Anthology of Syllabi.* Beverly Hills, Calif.: Sage Publications, 1968. 127 pp. Organized by topic. No index. Not annotated.

[28] DeConde, Alexander. *New Interpretations in American Foreign Policy.* 2d ed. (American Historical Association. Service Center for Teachers of History. Publication number 2.) Washington, D.C.: Service Center for Teachers of History, 1961. 43 pp. Interpretive essay. No index. Not annotated.

[29] *Foreign Affairs Bibliography; a Selected and Annotated List of Books on International Relations [1919-1962].* 4 vols. New York: Council on Foreign Relations, 1933-1964. Organized by topic. Index. Annotated.

Gaines. *Concealed Authorship.* (See 277)

Hays. *David Starr Jordan.* (See 475)

[30] Herman, Charles F., and Waltz, Kenneth N. *Basic Courses in Foreign Policy; an Anthology of Syllabi.* Beverly Hills, Calif.: Sage Publications, 1970. 117 pp. Organized by topic. No index. Not annotated.

Holler. *Sources of Political Science.* (See 268)

[31] Katz, Saul M., and McGowan, Frank. *A Selected List of U.S. Readings on Development.* Washington, D.C.: Agency for International Development, 1963. 363 pp. Organized by topic. Index. Annotated.

[32] Logan, Marguerite. *Geographical Bibliography for All the Major Nations of the World; Selected Books and Magazine Articles.* Ann Arbor, Mich.: Edwards, 1959. 396 pp. Organized by continent. No index. Not annotated.

[33] Plischke, Elmer. *American Foreign Relations; a Bibliography of Official Sources.* College Park: Bureau of Governmental Research, University of Maryland, 1955. 71 pp. Organized by topic. Index. Most items annotated.

[34] Ragatz, Lowell J., and Ragatz, Janet Evans. *A Bibliography of Articles, Descriptive, Historical and Scientific, on Colonies and other Dependent Territories, Appearing in American Geographical and Kindred Journals.* 2d ed. 2 vols. Washington, D.C.: Educational Research Bureau, 1951. Organized by topic. No index. Not annotated.

Slocum. *Biographical Dictionaries.* (See 10)

[35] U.S. Department of State. Historical Office. *Major Publications of the Department of State; an Annotated Bibliography.* (General Foreign Policy Series, number 200.) Washington, D.C.: G.P.O., 1966. 17 pp. Organized by topic. No index. Annotated.

[36] U.S. Department of State. Division of Publications. *Publications of the Department of State, October 1, 1929 to January 1, 1950.* Washington, D.C.: G.P.O., 1951. 136 pp. Supplements to December 31, 1960. Organized by topic. Index. Not annotated.

[37] U.S. Library of Congress. General Reference and Bibliography Division. *Current National Bibliographies.* Washington, D.C.: G.P.O., 1955. 132 pp. Organized by topic. Index. Annotated.

[38] U.S. Library of Congress. General Reference and Bibliography Division. *A Guide to Bibliographic Tools for Research in Foreign Affairs.* 2d ed., with supplement. Washington, D.C.: G.P.O., 1958. 145 pp. Organized by topic. Index. Annotated.

[39] Wilmington, S. Clay, and Sievers, Gale. *Complete Handbook on the Foreign Aid Policy of the United States. . . .* Skokie, Ill.: National Textbook, 1966. 239 pp. Organized by topic. No index. Annotated.

United States Relations With

Includes bibliographies which consider United States relations with continental geographic areas. See also: FOREIGN AFFAIRS: General & Miscellaneous; MILITARY: General & Miscellaneous, and Wars.

Europe

[40] Beers, Henry Putney. *The French in North America; a Bibliographical Guide to French Archives, Reproductions, and Research Missions.* Baton Rouge: Louisiana State University, 1957. 413 pp. Organized by type of publication. Index. Not annotated.

[41] U.S. Library of Congress. European Affairs Division. *The United States and Postwar Europe; a Bibliographical Examination of Thought Expressed in American Publications during 1948.* Washington, D.C.: G.P.O., 1948. 123 pp. Supplements, 1949; 1950; 1951-1952. Organized by topic. Index. Annotated.

Canada and Latin America

Cumberland. *U.S.-Mexican Border.* (See 148)

Harvard University. *Studies in Enterprise.* (See 57)

[42] Trask, David F., *et al. A Bibliography of United States-Latin American Relations since 1810.* Lincoln: University of Nebraska, 1968. 441 pp. Organized by topic. Index. Not annotated.

[43] U.S. Air Force Academy. Library. *The United States in the Caribbean.* (*Special Bibliography Series,* number 44.) Washington, D.C.: G.P.O., 1970. 34 pp. Organized by geographic region. No index. Not annotated.

Asia

Blanchard. *Korean War Bibliography.* (See 258)

[44] Ellinger, Werner B., and Rosinski, Herbert. *Sea Power in the Pacific, 1936-1941: a Selected Bibliography of Books, Periodical Articles and Maps from the End of the London Naval Conference to the Beginning of the War in the Pacific.* Princeton: Princeton University, 1947. 80 pp. Organized by topic. Index. Most items annotated.

[45] Horne, Norman P. *A Guide to Published United States Government Documents Pertaining to Southeast Asia, 1839-1941.* Washington,

D.C.: Catholic University of America, 1961. 147 pp. Organized by nation. No index. Not annotated.

[46] Liu, Kwang-Ching. *Americans and Chinese; a Historical Essay and Bibliography.* Cambridge, Mass.: Harvard University, 1963. 211 pp. Organized by topic. Index. Not annotated.

Other

[47] Hayton, Robert D. *National Interests in Antarctica, an Annotated Bibliography.* Washington, D.C.: G.P.O., 1959. 137 pp. Organized by nation. Index. Some items annotated.

Ragatz and Ragatz. *Colonies and Dependent Territories.* (See 34)

International Agencies, Peace Movements, & Disarmament

Includes bibliographies which consider attempts to abolish war, limit international hostilities, and stimulate international cooperation. See also: FOREIGN AFFAIRS: General & Miscellaneous; MILITARY: Wars.

[48] Cook, Blanche Wiesen. *Bibliography on Peace Research in History.* Santa Barbara, Calif.: ABC-Clio, 1969. 72 pp. Organized by topic. Index. Minority of items annotated.

[49] Gray, Charles Howard, *et al. A Bibliography of Peace Research Indexed by Key Words.* Eugene, Ore.: General Research Analysis Methods, 1968. 164 pp. Organized alphabetically. Full and complicated key-word index. Not annotated.

[50] Legault, Albert. *Peace-keeping Operations, Bibliography.* Paris, France: International Information Center on Peace-keeping Operations, 1967. 203 pp. Organized alphabetically by author. Poor index. Well annotated.

[51] Pickus, Robert, and Woito, Robert. *To End War: an Introduction to the Ideas, Books, Organizations, Work that Can Help.* Berkeley: World Without War Council, 1970. 261 pp. Organized by topic. Index. Annotated.

[52] U.S. Department of the Army. Army Library. *Disarmament: a Bibliographic Record, 1916-1960.* Washington, D.C.: G.P.O., 1960. Various pagings. Organized by topic. No index. Most items annotated.

3 / ECONOMICS

General & Miscellaneous

Includes bibliographies which consider introductions to economics as a subject and general United States economic development. Also included are bibliographies of subjects not considered in specific sections of Economics below. See also: POLITICS: Political Science & Miscellaneous, and Chronological & Elections; SOCIAL LIFE: Problems.

[53] Andreano, Ralph L., *et al. The Student Economist's Handbook: a Guide to Sources.* Cambridge, Mass.: Schenkman, 1967. 169 pp. Organized by topic. Index. Well annotated.

[54] Berry, Brian Joe Lobley, and Hankins, Thomas D. *A Bibliographic Guide to the Economic Regions of the United States.* Chicago: University of Chicago, Geography Department, 1963. 101 pp. Organized by topic. No index. Most items annotated.

Boston University. *New England Development.* (See 133)

Boston University. *State and Local Government.* (See 309)

[55] Cole, Arthur C. *Measure of Business Change; a Baker Library Index.* Chicago: Richard D. Irwin, 1952. 444 pp. Organized by topic. Index. Well annotated.

[56] Davis, Elizabeth Gould, *et al. Urbanization and Changing Land Use; a Bibliography of Selected References, 1950-1958.* (U.S. Department of Agriculture. *Miscellaneous Publications,* number 825.) Washington, D.C.: G.P.O., 1960. 212 pp. Organized by topic. Index. Annotated.

[57] Harvard University. Graduate School of Business Administration. Baker Library. *Studies in Enterprise: a Selected Bibliography of American and Canadian Company Histories and Biographies of Businessmen.* Boston: Author, 1957. 169 pp. Organized by topic. Index. Minority of items annotated.

[58] Larson, Henrietta M. *Guide to Business History; Materials for the Study of American Business History and Suggestions for their Use.* Cambridge, Mass.: Harvard University, 1948. 1,181 pp. Organized by topic. Index. Annotated.

[59] Lovett, Robert W. *American Economic and Business History Information Sources.* Detroit: Gale Research, 1971. 323 pp. Organized by topic. Index. Annotated.

[60] Melnyk, Peter. *Economics; Bibliographic Guide to Reference Book and Information Sources.* Littleton, Colo.: Libraries Unlimited, 1971. 263 pp. Organized by topic. Index. Annotated.

Mississippi. *Mississippi.* (See 178)

[61] Pittsburgh, University of. Department of Economics. *Cumulative Bibliography of Economics Books, 1954-1962.* New York: Gordon and Breach, 1965. 352 pp. Organized by topic. Index. Not annotated.

Powell. *Books of a New Nation.* (See 573)

Regional Economic Development Institute. *Regional Economic Development.* (See 294)

Social Science Research Council. *Civil-Military Relations.* (See 229)

Stewart. *Era of Franklin D. Roosevelt.* (See 576)

[62] Taylor, George Rogers. *American Economic History; Before 1860.* New York: Appleton-Century-Crofts, 1969. 108 pp. Organized by topic. Index. Not annotated.

Tennessee Valley Authority. *Program.* (See 296)

Turnbull. *Woodrow Wilson.* (See 22)

[63] U.S. Bureau of Land Management. *Public Lands Bibliography.* Washington, D.C.: G.P.O., 1962. 106 pp. Supplement, 1965. Organized by type of publication. No index. Not annotated.

U.S. Department of Health, Education and Welfare. *Grants-in-aid.* (See 299)

U.S. Library of Congress. General Reference and Bibliography Division. *Kennedy.* (See 16)

Theories & "Isms"

Includes bibliographies which consider various forms of economic theory, economic organization, and persons who were economic commentators or theorists. See also: POLITICS: Political Science & Miscellaneous, and Groups & Parties; SOCIAL LIFE: Problems.

Aptheker. *Student Rebellion.* (See 546)

[64] Bassett, T. D. Seymour. *Bibliography, Descriptive and Critical.* Vol. II of *Socialism in American Life* by Donald Drew Egbert and Stow Persons. 575 pp. 2 vols. Princeton: Princeton University, 1952. Organized by topic. Index. Annotated.

[65] California, University of, Davis. Library. *The American Communitarian Tradition, 1683-1940; a Guide to the Sources. . . .* Davis: Author, 1971. 88 pp. Organized by topic. No index. Not annotated.

Delaney. *Communism in America.* (See 274)

Ekirch. *Intellectual History.* (See 444)

Fisher. *Irving Fisher.* (See 471)

Fund for the Republic. *Communism.* (See 276)

Goldwater. *Radical Periodicals.* (See 278)

Johnson and Reeve. *Daniel De Leon.* (See 467)

Muller, *et al. Left to Right.* (See 279)

Seidman. *Communism in United States.* (See 280)

Texas. *Student Activism.* (See 281)

U.S. Congress. Senate. Committee on Government Operations. *Investigations of Communism.* (See 282)

U.S. National Agricultural Library. *Cooperation in Agriculture.* (See 78)

Agriculture

Includes bibliographies which consider plant and animal husbandry, cattle ranching, horticulture, forestry, water and soil conservation, government agricultural policies, and rural life. See also: ECONOMICS: Labor.

Adams. *Rampaging Herd.* (See 142)

[66] Anderson, Walfred A. *Bibliography of Researches in Rural Sociology.* Ithaca: New York State College of Agriculture, Cornell University, 1957. 186 pp. Organized by topic. Index. Not annotated.

[67] Banks, Vera. *Migration of Farm People: an Annotated Bibliography, 1946-1960.* (U.S. Department of Agriculture. *Miscellaneous Publications,* number 954.) Washington, D.C.: G.P.O., 1963. 37 pp. Organized by state. Index. Annotated.

[68] Bardolph, Richard. *Agricultural Literature and the Early Illinois Farmer.* Urbana: University of Illinois, 1948. 200 pp. Organized by type of publication. Index. Well annotated.

[69] Blanchard, J. Richard, and Ostvold, Harald. *Literature of Agricultural Research.* Berkeley: University of California, 1958. 231 pp. Organized by topic. Index. Most items annotated.

California. *Farm Migrant Education.* (See 551)

Edwards and Rasmussen. *Agriculture of Indians.* (See 375)

[70] Fite, Gilbert C. *American Agriculture and Farm Policy Since 1900.* (American Historical Association. Service Center for Teachers of History. Publication number 59.) Washington, D.C.: Service Center for Teachers of History, 1964. 28 pp. Interpretive essay. No index. Not annotated.

[71] Fundaburk, Emma Lida. *Reference Materials and Periodicals in Economics; an International List in Five Volumes.* Metuchen, N.J.: Scarecrow, 1971. (Vol. I: *Agriculture* published to date. 595 pp.) Organized by type of publication. Index. Not annotated.

Henefrund and Cummings. *Japanese in Agriculture.* (See 372)

[72] Jacobson, J. Myron, and Mersky, Roy M. *Water Law Bibliography, 1847-1965; Source Books on U.S. Water and Irrigation Studies.* Silver Spring, Md.: Jefferson Law Book, 1966. 246 pp. Supplement, 1967, 138 pp. Organized by topic. Index. Minority of items annotated.

[73] Manny, Elsie Sherman. *Rural Community Organization; Selected Annotated References.* Washington, D.C.: G.P.O., 1956. 124 pp. Organized by topic. Index. Annotated.

[74] Schlebecker, John T. *Bibliography of Books and Pamphlets on the History of Agriculture in the United States, 1607-1967.* Santa Barbara, Calif.: ABC-Clio, 1969. 183 pp. Organized alphabetically by author. Index. Minority of items annotated.

[75] Thompson, Edgar T. *The Plantation; a Bibliography.* Washington, D.C.: Pan American Union, 1957. 93 pp. Organized by topic. Index. Not annotated.

U.S. Department of Agriculture. *Agricultural Labor.* (See 110)

U.S. Department of Agriculture. *Farm Migration.* (See 111)

[76] U.S. Department of Agriculture. *Levels of Living of U.S. Farm Families; Selected Annotated References, 1940-1955. (Miscellaneous Publica-*

tions, number 746.) Washington, D.C.: G.P.O., 1957. 52 pp. Organized by date of publication. Index. Annotated.

[77] U.S. Department of Agriculture. Library. *Rural Community Organization, List of References.* (*Library List,* number 46.) Washington, D.C.: G.P.O., 1949. 51 pp. Organized by topic. Index. Annotated.

[78] U.S. National Agricultural Library. *Cooperation in Agriculture; 1954-1964: a List of Selected Periodicals.* (*Library List,* number 41, supplement 2.) Washington, D.C.: G.P.O., 1966. 115 pp. Organized by topic. Index. Minority of items annotated.

U.S. National Agricultural Library. *Low Income Farm People.* (See 117)

U.S. National Agricultural Library. *Migratory Labor.* (See 112)

Business

Includes bibliographies which consider general capitalistic enterprises (e.g., commerce, finance, public utilities). See also: ECONOMICS: General & Miscellaneous.

[79] Christian, Portia, and Hicks, Richard. *Ethics in Business Conduct: Selected References from the Record. . . .* Detroit: Gale Research, 1970. 155 pp. Organized by topic. Index. Annotated.

[80] Coman, Edwin T., Jr. *Sources of Business Information.* Rev. ed. Berkeley: University of California, 1964. 330 pp. Organized by topic. Index. Most items annotated.

[81] Cutlip, Scott M. *A Public Relations Bibliography.* 2d ed. Madison: University of Wisconsin, 1965. 305 pp. Organized by topic. Index. Annotated.

[82] Galambos, Louis. *American Business History.* (American Historical Association. Service Center for Teachers of History. Publication number 70.) Washington, D.C.: Service Center for Teachers of History, 1967. 32 pp. Interpretive essay. No index. Not annotated.

Harvard University. *Studies in Enterprise.* (See 57)

[83] Hunt, Florine E. *Public Utilities Information Sources; an Annotated Guide to Literature and Bodies Concerned with Rates, Economics, Accounting, Regulation, History and Statistics of Electric, Gas, Telephone and Water Companies.* Detroit: Gale Research, 1965. 200 pp. Organized by topic. Index. Annotated.

Lovett. *Economic and Business History.* (See 59)

[84] McDermott, Beatrice S., and Coleman, Freeda A. *Government Regulation of Business Including Antitrust: Information Sources; a Comprehensive Bibliography of Works. . . .* Detroit: Gale Research, 1967. 229 pp. Organized by topic. Index. Annotated.

Metzger. *Profit Sharing.* (See 101)

Michigan. *Automation.* (See 405)

Miller and Coghill. *Personnel Work.* (See 102)

Mundle. *Industrial Relations.* (See 103)

[85] Pittsburgh, University of. Bureau of Business Research. *Small Business Bibliography.* 2d ed. Pittsburgh: Author, 1958. 209 pp. Organized by topic. No index. Not annotated.

[86] Romaine, Lawrence B. *A Guide to American Trade Catalogs, 1744-1900.* New York: Bowker, 1960. 22 pp. Organized by topic. Index. Not annotated.

[87] Spear, Dorothea N. *Bibliography of American Directories Through 1860.* Worcester, Mass.: American Antiquarian Society, 1961. 389 pp. Organized alphabetically by communities. No index. Minority of items annotated.

Tompkins. *White Collar Crime.* (See 338)

U.S. Library of Congress. Map Division. *Marketing Maps.* (See 127)

Industry & Mining

Includes bibliographies which consider specific extractive and manufacturing industries. See also: ECONOMICS: Labor; SCIENCE: Technology.

Detroit. *Labor in the Automobile Industry.* (See 98)

Michigan. *Automation.* (See 405)

[88] Munn, Robert F. *The Coal Industry in America.* Morgantown: West Virginia University Library, 1965. 230 pp. Organized by topic. Index. Minority of items annotated.

[89] Swanson, Edward Benjamin. *A Century of Oil and Gas in Books, a Descriptive Bibliography.* New York: Appleton-Century-Crofts, 1960. 214 pp. Organized by topic. Index. Annotated.

Transportation

Includes bibliographies which consider such transportation facilities as railroads, ships, and pipelines, and government regulation of such facilities. See also: INTELLECTUAL & CULTURAL LIFE: Exploration & Travel; SCIENCE: General & Miscellaneous, and Technology.

[90] Ad Hoc Committee of Librarians for "Sources of Information in Transportation." *Sources of Information in Transportation.* Evanston, Ill.: Northwestern University, 1964. 262 pp. Organized by type of transportation. No index. Annotated.

[91] Albion, Robert Greenhalgh. *Naval and Maritime History; an Annotated Bibliography.* 3d ed., rev. and exp. Mystic, Conn.: Munson Institute of American Maritime History, 1963. 230 pp. 2 supplements. Organized by topic. Well indexed. Most items are annotated.

Bureau of Railway Economics. *In Defense and War.* (See 227)

[92] Flood, Kenneth U. *Research in Transportation: Legal/Legislative and Economic Sources and Procedure.* Detroit: Gale Research, 1970. 126 pp. Organized by type of publication. Index. Annotated.

Higham. *Maritime, Naval and Aeronautical History.* (See 263)

[93] Metcalf, Kenneth Nolan. *Transportation: Information Sources; an Annotated Guide to Publications, Agencies, and other Data Sources Concerning Air, Rail, Water, Road, and Pipeline Transportation.* Detroit: Gale Research, 1965. 307 pp. Organized by topic. Index. Annotated.

Port of New York Authority. *Bibliography of the Port Authority.* (See 223)

Renstrom. *Wilbur and Orville Wright.* (See 23)

[94] Siddall, William R. *Transportation Geography; a Bibliography.* Rev. ed. Manhattan: Kansas State University, 1967. 57 pp. Organized by topic. No index. Not annotated.

[95] Thompson, Thomas Richard. *Check List of Publications on American Railroads before 1841.* New York: New York Public Library, 1942. 250 pp. Organized by date of publication. Index. Minority of items annotated.

U.S. Library of Congress. Division of Aeronautics. *Aeronautic Americana.* (See 407)

U.S. Library of Congress. Map Division. *Explorers' Routes.* (See 426)

Labor

Includes bibliographies which consider free (not slave and not forced) labor, unions, employer-employee relations. Included are industrial, agricultural, commercial labor, and public employees. See also: ECONOMICS: Private Wealth & Poverty; POPULATION; SOCIAL LIFE: Problems.

[96] Blum, Albert A. *The Development of American Labor.* (American Historical Association. Service Center for Teachers of History. Publication number 48.) Washington, D.C.: Service Center for Teachers of History, 1963. 28 pp. Interpretive essay. No index. Not annotated.

California. *Farm Migrant Education.* (See 551)

[97] California, University of. Institute of Governmental Studies. *Strikes by Public Employees and Professional Personnel.* Berkeley: Author, 1967. 92 pp. Organized by topic. Index. Annotated.

[98] Detroit Public Library. *Labor Relations in the Automobile Industry; a Bibliography [Tracing developments . . . through the first four months of 1949].* Detroit: Author, 1950. 60 pp. Organized by type of publication. Index. Not annotated.

[99] Institute of Labor and Industrial Relations. University of Michigan-Wayne State University. *Document and Reference Text: an Index to Minority Group Employment Information.* Detroit: Wayne State University, 1967. 602 pp. Organized by topic (key word in context). Index. Not annotated.

[100] McCoy, Ralph Edward, and Gsell, Donald. *History of Labor and Unionism in the United States; a Selected Bibliography.* Urbana: Institute of Labor and Industrial Relations, University of Illinois, 1953. 88 pp. Organized alphabetically by author. Index. Not annotated.

[101] Metzger, Bertram L. *An Extensive, Indexed, Bibliography of American Publications on Profit Sharing Between 1940-1958.* Evanston, Ill.: Profit Sharing Research Foundation, 1959. 40 pp. Organized by type of publication. Index. Not annotated.

Michigan. *Automation.* (See 405)

[102] Miller, Frank B., and Coghill, Mary Ann. *The Historical Sources of Personnel Work, an Annotated Bibliography of Developments to 1923.* Ithaca: New York State School of Industrial and Labor

Relations, Cornell University, 1961. 110 pp. Organized by topic. Index. Annotated.

[103] Mundle, George F. *Industrial Relations Bibliographies; a Check-List.* Champaign: Institute of Labor and Industrial Relations, University of Illinois, 1965. 54 pp. Organized by date of publication. Index. Not annotated.

Munn. *Coal Industry.* (See 88)

[104] Neufeld, Maurice F. *A Representative Bibliography of American Labor History.* Ithaca: New York State School of Industrial and Labor Relations, Cornell University, 1964. 146 pp. Organized by topic. Index. Not annotated.

[105] Pendleton, Edwin C. *Labor in Hawaii, a Bibliography.* Honolulu: University of Hawaii, 1960. 62 pp. Organized by type of publication. No index. Not annotated.

[106] Rose, Fred Duane. *American Labor in Journals of History, a Bibliography.* Champaign: Institute of Labor and Industrial Relations, University of Illinois, 1962. 87 pp. Organized by journal. Index. Not annotated.

[107] Slobodeck, Mitchell. *A Selective Bibliography of California Labor History.* Los Angeles: Institute of Industrial Relations, University of California, Los Angeles, 1964. 265 pp. Organized by topic. Index. Some items annotated.

[108] Special Libraries Association. Social Science Group. *A Source List of Selected Labor Statistics.* Rev. ed. New York: Author, 1953. 113 pp. Organized by state and by topic. No index. Annotated.

[109] Stroud, Gene S., and Donahue, Gilbert E. *Labor History in the United States; a General Bibliography.* Urbana: University of Illinois, 1961. 167 pp. Organized alphabetically by author. Index. Not annotated.

U.S. Department of Agriculture. *Levels of Living.* (See 76)

[110] U.S. Department of Agriculture. Library. *Agricultural Labor in the United States, 1943-1952; a Selected List of Annotated References.* (*Library List*, number 61.) Washington, D.C.: G.P.O., 1954. 170 pp. Organized by topic. Index. Annotated.

[111] U.S. Department of Agriculture. Library. *Farm Migration, 1940-1945; an Annotated Bibliography.* (*Library List*, number 38.) Washington, D.C.: G.P.O., 1947. 51 pp. Organized alphabetically by author. Index. Annotated.

U.S. National Agricultural Library. *Low Income Farm People.* (See 117)

[112] U.S. National Agricultural Library. *Migratory Agricultural Labor in the United States; an Annotated Bibliography of Selected Sources.* (*Library List*, number 59.) Washington, D.C.: G.P.O., 1953. 64 pp. Organized by topic. Index. Annotated.

Private Wealth & Poverty

Includes bibliographies which consider the distribution of economic wealth in the United States and the economic problems of various social groups (e.g., elderly people, ethnic, racial). Emphasis of references here is to poverty and to limited economic wealth. See also: ECONOMICS: Labor; POPULATION; SOCIAL LIFE: Problems.

Banks. *Migration of Farm People.* (See 67)

Booth, *et al. Culturally Disadvantaged.* (See 549)

Bracket, *et al. Social Stratification.* (See 550)

California. *Farm Migrant Education.* (See 551)

Dunmore. *Poverty, Participation, Protest.* (See 554)

[113] Institute for Rural America. *Poverty; Rural Poverty and Minority Groups Living in Rural Poverty: an Annotated Bibliography.* Lexington, Ky.: Spindletop Research, 1969. 159 pp. Organized by topic. No index. Annotated.

Institute of Labor and Industrial Relations. *Minority Group Employment.* (See 99)

Potter. *Health and Illness in New Mexico.* (See 563)

[114] Schlesinger, Benjamin. *Poverty in Canada and the United States; Overview and Annotated Bibliography.* Toronto, Ont.: University of Toronto, 1966. 211 pp. Organized by topic. Index. Annotated.

Snodgrass. *Indians and Eskimos.* (See 382)

[115] Tompkins, Dorothy C. *Poverty in the United States During the Sixties.* Berkeley: Institute of Governmental Studies, University of California, 1970. 542 pp. Organized by topic. Index. Not annotated.

U.S. Administration on Aging. *Words on Aging.* (See 527)

U.S. Department of Agriculture. *Agricultural Labor.* (See 110)

U.S. Department of Agriculture. *Farm Migration.* (See 111)

U.S. Department of Agriculture. *Levels of Living.* (See 76)

[116] U.S. Department of Health, Education and Welfare. Library. *Basic Readings in Social Security; 25th Anniversary of the Social Security Act, 1935-1960.* Washington, D.C.: G.P.O., 1960. 221 pp. Organized by topic. Index. Most items annotated.

[117] U.S. National Agricultural Library. *Low Income Farm People; a Selected List of References.* (*Library List*, number 62.) Washington, D.C.: G.P.O., 1955. 46 pp. Organized by topic. Index. Annotated.

U.S. National Agricultural Library. *Migratory Labor.* (See 112)

[118] U.S. Social Security Administration. Office of Research and Statistics. *Poverty Studies in the Sixties; a Selected, Annotated Bibliography.* Washington, D.C.: G.P.O., 1970. 126 pp. Organized by topic. Index. Annotated.

U.S. Special Staff for Employee Management Relations and Equal Employment Opportunities. *Not Just Some of Us.* (See 564)

Statistics

Includes bibliographies which consider statistical material compiled by private and government sources. Much statistical material is related to economic data; therefore, such forms of information are listed here. But the researcher should recognize that statistical information may sometimes be related to political or social phenomena. See also: ECONOMICS: General & Miscellaneous, and Private Wealth & Poverty; POPULATION: Vital Statistics; POLITICS: Political Science & Miscellaneous; SOCIAL LIFE: Problems.

Sirken. *Life Tables.* (See 390)

Special Libraries Association. *Labor Statistics.* (See 108)

[119] Wasserman, Paul, *et al. Statistics Sources; a Subject Guide to Data on Industrial, Business, Social, Educational, Financial, and Other Topics for the United States and Foreign Countries.* 2d ed. Detroit: Gale Research, 1965. 387 pp. Organized by topic. No index. Not annotated.

4 / GEOGRAPHY & LOCAL HISTORY

General, Miscellaneous, & Cartography

Includes bibliographies which consider the geography and maps of the United States. Bibliographies here emphasize demographic, economic, and/or political factors. See also: ECONOMICS: Transportation; GEOGRAPHY & LOCAL HISTORY: Sections, and Parts of States; POPULATION; INTELLECTUAL & CULTURAL LIFE: Exploration & Travel.

Albion. *Naval and Maritime History.* (See 91)

[120] Church, Martha, *et al. A Basic Geographical Library: a Selected and Annotated Book List for American Colleges.* Washington, D.C.: Association of American Geographers, 1966. 153 pp. Organized by topic. Index. Annotated.

[121] Logasa, Hannah. *Regional United States; a Subject List.* Boston: F.W. Faxon, 1942. 71 pp. Organized by topic. Index. Not annotated.

[122] McManis, Douglas R. *Historical Geography of the United States; a Bibliography—Excluding Alaska and Hawaii.* Ypsilanti: Eastern Michigan University, 1965. 249 pp. Organized by region. No index. Not annotated.

Peterson. *County Histories.* (See 222)

[123] Petsche, Jerome E. *Bibliography of Salvage Archeology in the United States.* Lincoln, Nebr.: Smithsonian Institute, 1968. 162 pp. Organized by state and geographic area. Index. Not annotated.

[124] Sealock, Richard Burl, and Seely, Pauline Augusta. *Bibliography of Place-Name Literature; United States and Canada.* 2d ed. Chicago: American Library Association, 1967. 352 pp. Organized by state and region. Index. Most items annotated.

Siddall. *Transportation Geography.* (See 94)

U.S. Library of Congress. Geography and Map Division. *County Maps.* (See 224)

[125] U.S. Library of Congress. Map Division. *A Descriptive List of Treasure Maps and Charts. . . .* Washington, D.C.: G.P.O., 1964. 29 pp. Organized by type of publication. Index. Annotated.

[126] U.S. Library of Congress. Map Division. *A List of Atlases in the Library of Congress; with Bibliographical Notes (A Continuation of Four Volumes by Philip Lee Phillips).* Washington, D.C.: G.P.O., 1958 and 1963. Volumes 5 and 6. Organized by topic. Index. Annotated.

U.S. Library of Congress. Map Division. *Explorers' Routes.* (See 426)

[127] U.S. Library of Congress. Map Division. *Marketing Maps of the United States; an Annotated Bibliography.* 3d rev. ed. Washington, D.C.: G.P.O., 1958. 147 pp. Organized by type of publication. Index. Annotated.

[128] U.S. Library of Congress. Map Division. *United States Atlases; a List of National, State, County, City, and Regional Atlases in the Library of Congress.* Washington, D.C.: G.P.O., 1950. 445 pp. Organized by community. No index. Not annotated.

U.S. National Archives. *Civil War Maps.* (See 252)

[129] Vinge, Clarence L., and Vinge, Ada Grace. *U.S. Government Publications for Research and Teaching in Geography and Related Social and Natural Sciences.* Norman, Okla.: National Council for Geographic Education, 1961. 105 pp. Organized by issuing department of the federal government. No index. Not annotated.

[130] Wheat, James Clement, and Brun, Christian F. *Maps and Charts Published in America Before 1800; a Bibliography.* New Haven: Yale University, 1969. 215 pp. Organized by topic. Index. Annotated.

[131] Wright, John Kirtland, and Platt, Elizabeth T. *Aids to Geographical Research; Bibliographies, Periodicals, Atlases, Gazetteers, and Other Reference Books.* 2d ed. New York: Columbia University, 1947. 331 pp. Organized by topic. Index. Most items annotated.

Sections

Includes bibliographies which consider economic, political, and/or general historical material on various sections of the United States. The subcategories below describe the various sections for the purpose of this guide. See also: ECONOMICS: Transportation; GEOGRAPHY & LOCAL HISTORY: General, Miscellaneous, & Cartography; POPULATION; INTELLECTUAL & CULTURAL LIFE: Exploration & Travel.

North: New England, Middle Atlantic, Old Northwest

Beers. *The French.* (See 40)

[132] Beers, Henry Putney. *The French and British in the Old Northwest; a Bibliographical Guide to Archive and Manuscript Sources.* Detroit: Wayne State University, 1964. 297 pp. Organized by topic. Index. Well annotated.

[133] Boston University. Area Development Center. *New England Development Bibliography.* Washington, D.C.: U.S. Department of Commerce, 1966. 437 pp. Organized by topic. No index. Not annotated.

[134] Cone, Gertrude. *Selective Bibliography of Publications on the Champlain Valley.* Plattsburgh, N.Y.: New York-Vermont Interstate Commission

on the Lake Champlain Basin, 1959. 144 pp. Organized alphabetically by author. Index. Most items annotated.

Hubach. *Early Midwestern Travel.* (See 423)

Port of New York Authority. *Bibliography of the Port.* (See 223)

[135] Stevens, Harry Robert. *The Middle West.* 2d ed. (American Historical Association. Service Center for Teachers of History. Publication number 12.) Washington, D.C.: Service Center for Teachers of History, 1965. 26 pp. Interpretive essay. No index. Not annotated.

[136] Vail, Robert William G. *The Voice of the Old Frontier.* Philadelphia: University of Pennsylvania, 1949. 492 pp. Organized by date of publication. Index. Annotated.

South: States of the Civil War Confederacy (Except for Texas)

Beers. *Government of the Confederate States.* (See 234)

[137] Boger, Loris C. *The Southern Mountaineer in Literature; an Annotated Bibliography.* Morgantown: West Virginia University Library, 1964. 105 pp. Organized alphabetically by author. Index. Annotated.

Coulter. *Confederate States.* (See 422)

Crandall. *Confederate Imprints.* (See 236)

Fishwick and Hollis. *R.E. Lee.* (See 239)

Harwell. *More Confederate Imprints.* (See 240)

McMillan. *Southern Speech.* (See 497)

[138] Munn, Robert F. *The Southern Appalachians; a Bibliography and Guide to Studies.* Morgantown: West Virginia University Library, 1961. 106 pp. Organized by topic. Index. Not annotated.

Rubin. *Southern Literature.* (See 460)

[139] Singletary, Otis A., and Bailey, Kenneth K. *The South in American History.* 2d ed. (American Historical Association. Service Center for Teachers of History. Publication number 3.) Washington, D.C.: Service Center for Teachers of History, 1965. 27 pp. Interpretive essay. No index. Not annotated.

[140] Steck, Francis Borgia. *A Tentative Guide to Historical Materials on the Spanish Borderlands.* New York: Burt Franklin, 1971 (reprint of 1943 edition). 106 pp. Organized by geographic section. No index. Some items annotated.

Tennessee Valley Authority. *Program.* (See 296)

Thompson and Thompson. *Race and Region.* (See 319)

Thompson. *Southern Black.* (See 359)

West: Trans-Mississippi Valley to Rocky Mountains & Bibliographies Which Consider Frontier Movement (Excludes Far Southwest & Northwest)

[141] Adams, Ramon Frederick. *Burs under the Saddle, a Second Look at Books and Histories of the West.* Norman: University of Oklahoma, 1964. 610 pp. Organized alphabetically by author. Index. Well annotated.

[142] Adams, Ramon Frederick. *The Rampaging Herd; a Bibliography of Books and Pamphlets on Men and Events in the Cattle Industry.* Norman: University of Oklahoma, 1959. 463 pp. Organized alphabetically by author. Index. Minority of items annotated.

[143] Adams, Ramon Frederick. *Six-Guns and Saddle Leather; a Bibliography of Books and Pamphlets on Western Outlaws and Gunmen.* New ed., rev. and enl. Norman: University of Oklahoma, 1969. 808 pp. Organized alphabetically by author. Index. Most items annotated.

[144] Billington, Ray Allen. *The American Frontier.* 2d ed. (American Historical Association. Service Center for Teachers of History. Publication number 8.) Washington, D.C.: Service Center for Teachers of History, 1965. 44 pp. Interpretive essay. No index. Not annotated.

Carter. *The Far West.* (See 154)

Jacobson and Mersky. *Water Law.* (See 72)

[145] Jannewein, J. Leonard. *Black Hills Booktrails.* Mitchell, S. Dak.: Dakota Territory Centennial Commission and Dakota Wesleyan University, 1962. 111 pp. Organized by topic. Index. Annotated.

Jonas. *Western Politics.* (See 269)

[146] McVicker, Mary Louise. *The Writings of J. Frank Dobie; a Bibliography.* Lawton, Okla.: Museum of the Great Plains, 1968. 258 pp. Organized by type of publication. Index. Not annotated.

Wagner. *Plains and Rockies.* (See 427)

[147] Winther, Oscar Osburn. *A Classified Bibliography of the Periodical Literature of the Trans-Mississippi West (1811-1951).* Bloomington: Indiana University, 1961. 626 pp. Supplement, 1957-1970, 340 pp. Organized by topic. Index. Not annotated.

Southwest: Texas, Oklahoma, and Beyond

[148] Cumberland, Charles Curtis. *The United States-Mexican Border; a Selective Guide to the Literature of the Region.* Ithaca, N.Y.: Rural Sociology Society, 1960. [Originally a supplement to *Rural Sociology* XXV, no. 2 (June 1960).] 236 pp. Organized by topic. Index. Annotated.

[149] Dobie, J. Frank. *Guide to Life and Literature of the Southwest.* Rev. ed. Dallas, Tex.: Southern Methodist University, 1952. 222 pp. Organized by topic. Index. Annotated.

Dykes. *Billy the Kid.* (See 13)

[150] Edwards, Elza Ivan. *The Enduring Desert; a Descriptive Bibliography.* Los Angeles: Ward Ritchie, 1969. 306 pp. Organized alphabetically by author. Index. Annotated.

[151] Farquhar, Francis P. *The Books of the Colorado River & the Grand Canyon; a Selective Bibliography.* Los Angeles: Glen Dawson, 1953. 75 pp. Organized by topic. Index. Annotated.

[152] Rader, Jesse L. *South of Forty from the Mississippi to the Rio Grande, a Bibliography.* Norman: University of Oklahoma, 1947. 336 pp. Organized alphabetically by author. Index. Minority of items annotated.

[153] Rittenhouse, Jack DeVire. *The Santa Fe Trail; a Historical Bibliography.* Albuquerque: University of New Mexico, 1971. 271 pp. Organized alphabetically by author. Index. Annotated.

Steck. *Spanish Borderlands.* (See 140)

Far West: Pacific Coast States

[154] Carter, Harvey L. *The Far West in American History.* 2d ed. (American Historical Association. Service Center for Teachers of History. Publication number 26.) Washington, D.C.: Service Center for Teachers of History, 1964. 25 pp. Interpretive essay. No index. Not annotated.

[155] Inland Empire Council of Teachers of English. *Northwest Books.* Portland, Ore.: Binfords & Mort, 1942. 356 pp. Supplement, 1949, 278 pp. Lincoln: University of Nebraska. Organized alphabetically by author. Index. Annotated.

[156] Smith, Charles Wesley. *Pacific Northwest Americana; a Check List of Books and Pamphlets Relating to the History of the Pacific Northwest.* 3d ed., rev. and ext. Portland, Ore.: Binfords & Mort,

1950. 381 pp. Organized alphabetically by author. No index. Not annotated.

States (by Name)

Includes bibliographies which consider the various states individually. Arranged alphabetically by state. See also: ECONOMICS: General & Miscellaneous, and Transportation; GEOGRAPHY & LOCAL HISTORY: General, Miscellaneous, & Cartography; POLITICS: State Government; INTELLECTUAL & CULTURAL LIFE: Exploration & Travel.

[157] Lada-Mocarski, Valerian. *Bibliography of Books on Alaska Published Before 1868.* New Haven: Yale University, 1969. 567 pp. Organized by date of publication. Index. Annotated.

[158] Tekesky, Pauline. *Seward's Folly; the Story of Alaska.* Chapel Hill: University of North Carolina, 1960. 32 pp. Organized by topic. No index. Annotated.

[159] Powell, Donald M. *An Arizona Gathering; a Bibliography of Arizoniana, 1950-1959.* Tucson: Arizona Pioneers' Historical Society, 1960. 77 pp. Organized alphabetically by author. Index. Not annotated.

[160] Wallace, Andrew. *Sources & Readings in Arizona History.* Tucson: Arizona Pioneer Historical Society, 1965. 181 pp. Organized by topic. Author index. Not annotated.

California, University of. *Japanese American Evacuation.* (See 369)

Cogan. *Pioneer Jews of the California Mother Lode.* (See 536)

Hansen and Heintz. *Chinese in California.* (See 371)

[161] Leuthold, David A. *California Politics and Problems, 1900-1963; a Selective Bibliography.* Berkeley: University of California, 1969. 64 pp. Supplement, 1969. Organized by topic. Index. Not annotated.

Slobodeck. *California Labor History.* (See 107)

[162] Stern, Norton B. *California Jewish History; a Descriptive Bibliography: Over Five Hundred Fifty Works for the Period Gold Rush to Post World War I.* Glendale, Calif.: A.H. Clark, 1967. 175 pp. Organized alphabetically by author. Index. Annotated.

[163] Weber, Francis J. *A Bibliography of California Bibliographies.* Los Angeles: Ward Ritchie, 1968. 39 pp. Organized alphabetically by author. No index. Annotated.

Weber. *California Catholic History.* (See 535)

[164] Wilcox, Virginia Lee. *Colorado: a Selected Bibliography of its Literature, 1858-1952.* Denver, Colo.: Sage Books, 1954. 151 pp. Organized alphabetically by author. Index. Briefly annotated.

[165] Reed, Henry Clay, and Reed, Marion B. *A Bibliography of Delaware Through 1960.* Newark: University of Delaware, 1966. 196 pp. Organized by topic. Index. Minority of items annotated.

[166] Hanna, A. J. *Recommended Readings on Florida.* Winter Park, Fla.: Union Catalog of Floridiana, 1946. 64 pp. Organized by topic. Index. Annotated.

[167] Rowland, Arthur Ray. *A Bibliography of the Writings on Georgia History.* Hamden, Conn.: Shoestring, 1966. 289 pp. Organized alphabetically by author. Index. Minority of items annotated.

Pendleton. *Labor in Hawaii.* (See 105)

[168] Rubano, Judith. *Culture and Behavior in Hawaii.* Honolulu: Social Science Research Institute, University of Hawaii, 1971. 147 pp. Organized alphabetically by author. Index. Annotated.

[169] Idaho Historical Society. *A List of References for Idaho History.* Boise: Author, 1959. Unpaged. Organized by region of the state. No index. Most items annotated.

Bardolph. *Agricultural Literature and the Early Illinois Farmer.* (See 68)

[170] Peterson, William J. *Iowa History Reference Guide.* Iowa City: State Historical Society of Iowa, 1952. 192 pp. Organized by topic. Index. Not annotated.

[171] Coleman, J. Winston, Jr. *A Bibliography of Kentucky History.* Lexington: University of Kentucky, 1949. 516 pp. Organized by topic. Index. Annotated.

[172] Jillson, Willard Rouse. *Books on Kentucky Books and Writers; a Bibliography, 1784-1950.* Frankfort, Ky.: Roberts Books, 1951. 27 pp. Organized alphabetically by author. No index. Annotated.

[173] Alabama, University of. Library. *A Bibliography of Louisiana Books and Pamphlets. . . .* n.p.: Author, 1947. 210 pp. Organized by topic. Index. Minority of items annotated.

[174] *The Louisiana Union Catalog.* Baton Rouge: Louisiana Library Association, 1960. 912 pp. Supplement, 1959-1962. Organized alphabetically by author and title. No index. Not annotated.

[175] Bangor Public Library. *Bibliography of the State of Maine.* Boston: G.K. Hall, 1962. 803 pp. Organized alphabetically by author and title. No index. Not annotated.

[176] Detroit Public Library. *Michigan in Books.* Detroit: Author, 1956. 63 pp. Organized by topic. No index. Annotated.

[177] Greenly, Albert Harry. *A Selective Bibliography of Important Books, Pamphlets, and Broadsides Relating to Michigan History.* Lunenburg, Vt.: Stinehour, 1958. 165 pp. Organized by topic. Index. Annotated.

May. *Michigan Civil War.* (See 242)

[178] Mississippi, University of. Bureau of Governmental Research. *An Annotated Bibliography on Mississippi's Economy, Business, Industry, and Government, 1930-1963.* Oxford: Author, 1964. 259 pp. Organized by topic. Index. Annotated.

[179] Elliot, Russell R., and Poulton, Helen J. *Writings on Nevada; a Selected Bibliography.* Reno: University of Nevada, 1963. 156 pp. Organized by author. Index. Not annotated.

Bibliography Committee of the New Jersey Library Association. *New Jersey and the Negro.* (See 347)

[180] Burr, Nelson R. *A Narrative and Descriptive Bibliography of New Jersey.* Princeton: Van Nostrand, 1964. 265 pp. Organized by topic. Index. Well annotated.

Sinclair. *Civil War and New Jersey.* (See 248)

Potter. *Health and Illness in New Mexico.* (See 563)

Rittenhouse. *New Mexico Civil War.* (See 246)

[181] Saunders, Lyle. *A Guide to Materials Bearing on Cultural Relations in New Mexico.* Albuquerque: University of New Mexico, 1944. 528 pp. Organized by topic. Index. Minority of items annotated.

[182] Breuer, Ernest Henry. *Constitutional Development in New York, 1777-1958; a Bibliography.* (New York State Library. *Bibliography Bulletin,* number 82.) Albany: New York State Library, 1958. 103 pp. Organized by topic. No index. Minority of items annotated.

[183] Lefler, Hugh Talmage. *A Guide to the Study and Reading of North Carolina History.* 3d ed. Chapel Hill: University of North Carolina, 1969. 280 pp. Organized by topic. No index. Not annotated.

[184] Thornton, Mary Lindsay. *A Bibliography of North Carolina, 1589-1956.* Chapel Hill: University of North Carolina, 1958. 597 pp. Organized alphabetically by author. Index. Not annotated.

Hostetler. *Bibliography on Amish.* [Pennsylvania] (See 544)

[185] Pennsylvania Historical and Museum Commission. *Bibliography of Pennsylvania History.* 2d ed. Harrisburg: Author, 1957. 826 pp. Organized by topic. Index. Minority of items annotated.

[186] Pennsylvania Historical and Museum Commission. *Guide to the Published Archives of Pennsylvania; Covering the 138 Volumes of Colonial Records and Pennsylvania Archives, Series, I-IX.* Harrisburg: Author, 1949. 101 pp. Poorly organized by topic. No index. Not annotated.

[187] Cohen, Hennig. *Articles in Periodicals and Serials on South Carolina Literature and Related Subjects, 1900-1955.* Columbia: South Carolina Archives, 1956. 87 pp. Organized by topic. Index. Not annotated.

[188] Easterby, James Harold. *Guide to the Study and Reading of South Carolina History.* Provisional edition. 2 pts. Columbia: Historical Commission of South Carolina, 1953. Organized by topic. Index. Not annotated.

[189] Jones, Lewis P. *Books and Articles on South Carolina History.* Columbia: University of South Carolina, 1970. 102 pp. Organized by topic. No index. Annotated.

[190] Petty, Julian J. *A Bibliography of the Geography of the State of South Carolina.* Columbia: University of South Carolina, 1952. 126 pp. Organized alphabetically by author. Index. Not annotated.

[191] Turnbull, Robert James. *Bibliography of South Carolina, 1563-1950.* 6 vols. Charlottesville: University of Virginia, 1956-1960. Organized by date of publication. Index. Minority of items annotated.

[192] Parmelee, Gertrude. *A South Dakota Bibliography.* Rapid City: South Dakota Library Association, 1960. 33 pp. Organized by topic. Index. Annotated.

[193] Alderson, William Thomas, and White, Robert H. *A Guide to the Study and Reading of Tennessee History.* Nashville: Tennessee Historical Commission, 1959. 87 pp. Organized by topic. No index. Not annotated.

[194] Allen, Ronald R. *Tennessee Books; a Preliminary Guide.* Knoxville, Tenn.: n.p., 1969. 63 pp. Organized alphabetically by author. Index. Not annotated.

[195] Streeter, Thomas Winthrop. *Bibliography of Texas; 1795-1845.* 5 vols. Cambridge, Mass.: Harvard University, 1955-1960. Organized by date of publication. Index. Annotated.

[196] Texas, University of. Institute of Public Affairs. *Bibliography on Texas Government.* Rev. ed. Austin: Author, 1964. 194 pp. Organized by topic. No index. Not annotated.

Brigham Young University. *Works on Mormonism.* (See 539)

[197] Kirkpatrick, L.H. *Holdings of the University of Utah on Utah and the Church of Jesus Christ of Latter-day Saints.* Salt Lake City: University of Utah, 1954. 285 pp. Organized by topic. No index. Not annotated.

Bear and Bear. *Virginia Almanacs.* (See 503)

Washington. *Negro in Washington.* (See 362)

U.S. Library of Congress. General Reference and Bibliography Division. *Capitol.* [Washington, D.C.] (See 307)

U.S. Library of Congress. General Reference and Bibliography Division. *White House.* [Washington, D.C.] (See 308)

[198] Munn, Robert F. *Index to West Virginiana.* Charleston, W. Va.: Education Foundation, 1960. 154 pp. Organized alphabetically by author and topic. No index. Not annotated.

Shetler. *West Virginia Civil War Literature.* (See 247)

[199] Schlinkert, Leroy. *Subject Bibliography of Wisconsin History.* Madison: Wisconsin Historical Society, 1947. 213 pp. Organized by topic. No index. Not annotated.

[200] Malone, Rose Mary. *Wyomingana; Two Bibliographies.* Denver: University of Denver, 1950. 66 pp. Organized alphabetically by author. No index. Most items annotated.

Parts of States (by Name)

Includes bibliographies which consider counties, towns, and other substate divisions specifically by name. Arranged alphabetically by state in which the community is located. See also: GEOGRAPHY & LOCAL HISTORY: States (by Name).

[201] Adams, John. *Books and Authors of San Diego; a Check List.* San Diego: San Diego State College, 1966. 250 pp. Organized alphabetically by author. Index. Not annotated.

[202] Rocq, Margaret Miller. *California Local History; a Bibliography and Union List of Library Holdings.* 2d ed., rev. and enl. Stanford: Stanford University, 1970. 611 pp. Organized by topic. Index. Not annotated.

[203] San Diego 200th Anniversary, Inc. Historical Research, Archival Material, Libraries Committee. *San Diego, California, a Bicentennial Bibliography, 1769-1969.* San Diego: Author, 1969. 287 pp. Organized alphabetically by author. No index. Not annotated.

[204] Weber, Francis J. *A Select Los Angeles Bibliography, 1872-1970.* Los Angeles: Dawson's Book Shop, 1970. 44 pp. Organized alphabetically by author. No index. Annotated.

[205] Wheat, Carl I. *Books of the California Gold Rush.* San Francisco: Colt, 1949. Unpaged. Organized alphabetically by author. Index. Annotated.

[206] Rowland, Arthur Ray. *A Guide to the Study of Augusta and Richmond County, Georgia.* Augusta: Richmond County Historical Society, 1967. 69 pp. Organized alphabetically by author. Index. Minority of items annotated.

[207] Jillson, Willard Rouse. *A Bibliography of Mammoth Cave, 1789-1949.* Frankfort, Ky.: Roberts Printing, 1953. 81 pp. Organized by date of publication. No index. Annotated.

[208] Jillson, Willard Rouse. *An Historical Bibliography of Lexington, Kentucky, 1774-1946.* Frankfort, Ky.: Perry, 1947. 107 pp. Organized by date of publication. No index. Annotated.

[209] *Adirondack Bibliography; a List of Books, Pamphlets and Periodical Articles Published through the Year 1955.* [New York] Gabriels, N.Y.: Adirondack Mountain Club, 1958. 354 pp. Organized by topic. Index. Minority of items annotated.

Bailey. *Genealogical and Biographical Sources.* [New York City] (See 1)

[210] Cole, G. Glyndon, and Plum, Dorothy A. *Historical Materials Relating to Northern New York; a Union Catalog.* Plattsburgh, N.Y.: North County Reference and Research Resources Council, 1968. 307 pp. Organized by topic. Index. Not annotated.

[211] Eiberson, Harold. *Sources for the Study of the New York Area.* New York: Institute of New York Area Studies, City College of New York, 1960. 128 pp. Organized by topic. Index. Well annotated.

[212] Nestler, Harold. *A Bibliography of New York State Communities, Counties, Towns, Villages.* New York: I.J. Friedman, 1968. Unpaged [103 pp.]. Organized by county. Index. Not annotated.

[213] Parker, Ted F., and Parker, Virginia E. *Local Government in New York State During the Dutch Period.* Albany, N.Y.: Government Affairs Foundation, 1968. 41 pp. Organized alphabetically by author. Index. Annotated.

Port of New York Authority. *Bibliography of the Port.* (See 223)

[214] Powell, William S. *North Carolina County Histories; a Bibliography.* (University of North Carolina, *Library Studies,* number 1.) Chapel Hill: University of North Carolina Library, 1958. 27 pp. Organized by county. No index. Not annotated.

Jannewein. *Black Hills Booktrails.* (See 145)

[215] Carroll, H. Bailey. *Texas County Histories; a Bibliography.* Austin: Texas State Historical Association, 1943. 200 pp. Organized by county. Index. Not annotated.

[216] Jenkins, John Holmes. *Cracker Barrel Chronicles; a Bibliography of Texas Town and County Histories.* Austin: Pemberton, 1965. 509 pp. Organized by county. Index. Not annotated.

Carson. *Tidewater Virginia.* (See 419)

Parts of States (General)

Includes bibliographies which consider counties, towns, and other substate divisions. Only those bibliographies which consider general community life are included. See also: ECONOMICS: Private Wealth & Poverty; POLITICS: Public Administration, and State Government; SOCIAL LIFE: Problems.

[217] Bollens, John C., *et al. American County Government, with an Annotated Bibliography.* Beverly Hills, Calif.: Sage Publications, 1969. 433 pp. Organized by topic. Index. Annotated.

Boston University. *State and Local Government in New England.* (See 309)

California, University of, Davis. *Communitarian Tradition.* (See 65)

[218] Child, Sargent Burrage, and Holmes, Dorothy P. *Check List of Historical Records Survey Publications; Bibliography of Research Projects Reports.* Reprint of 1943 ed. Baltimore: Genealogical Publishing, 1969. 110 pp. Organized by topic. No index. Not annotated.

Davis, *et al. Urbanization and Changing Land Use.* (See 56)

[219] Government Affairs Foundation, New York. *Metropolitan Communities; a Bibliography with Special Emphasis upon Government and Politics.*

Chicago: Public Administration Service, 1957. 392 pp. Supplements: 1960; 1967; 1969. Organized by topic. Index. Some items annotated.

Meyer. *Urban Crisis.* (See 561)

[220] Michigan State University, East Lansing. Institute for Community Development and Service. *Main Street Politics: Policy-Making at the Local Level, a Survey of the Periodical Literature Since 1950.* East Lansing: Author, 1962. 147 pp. Organized by topic. Index. Annotated.

[221] Payne, Raymond, and Bailey, Wilfred C. *The Community; a Classified Annotated Bibliography.* Athens: University of Georgia, 1967. 142 pp. Organized by topic. Index. Annotated.

[222] Peterson, Clarence S. *Consolidated Bibliography of County Histories in Fifty States in 1961, Consolidated 1935-1961.* Baltimore: Genealogical Publishing, 1963. 186 pp. Organized by state and county. No index. Not annotated.

[223] Port of New York Authority. *A Selected Bibliography of the Port of New York Authority, 1921-1968.* Rev. of 1965 ed. New York: Author, 1969. 81 pp. Organized by topic. No index. Not annotated.

U.S. Air Force Academy. Library. *The States and the Urban Crisis.* (See 315)

U.S. Department of Agriculture. *Community Organization.* (See 77)

[224] U.S. Library of Congress. Geography and Map Division. *Land Ownership Maps, a Checklist of Nineteenth Century United States County Maps. . . .* Washington, D.C.: G.P.O., 1967. 86 pp. Organized by state. Index. Not annotated.

5 / MILITARY

General & Miscellaneous

Includes bibliographies which consider military policy, military-civil relations, guerrilla and psychological warfare, veterans' affairs, and other general types of military activities. See also: FOREIGN AFFAIRS: General & Miscellaneous, and United States Relations With.

American University. *Psychological Operations.* (See 24)

[225] American University. Special Operations Research Office. *A Counterinsurgency Bibliography.* Washington, D.C.: Author, 1963. 333 pp. Supplements to 1966. Organized by topic. Index. Annotated.

[226] American University. Special Operations Research Office. *A Selected Bibliography on Unconventional Warfare.* Washington, D.C.: Author, 1961. 123 pp. Supplements to 1965. Organized by topic. Index. Annotated.

[227] Bureau of Railway Economics. *Railroads in Defense and War; a Bibliography.* Washington, D.C.: Association of American Railroads, 1953. 262 pp. Organized by topic. Index. Minority of items annotated.

Legault. *Peace-keeping Operations.* (See 50)

[228] Millis, Walter. *Military History.* (American Historical Association. Service Center for Teachers of History. Publication number 39.) Washington, D.C.: Service Center for Teachers of History, 1961. 18 pp. Interpretive essay. No index. Not annotated.

[229] Social Science Research Council. Committee on Civil-Military Relations Research. *Civil-Military Relations, an Annotated Bibliography, 1940-1952.* New York: Columbia University, 1954. 140 pp. Organized by topic. Index. Annotated.

U.S. Veterans Administration. Medical and General Reference Library. *Care of the Veteran.* (See 400)

Wars

Includes bibliographies which consider wars fought by Americans, from colonial times to the present. Arranged in chronological order. Almost all bibliographies consider political, social, and economic (nonmilitary) civilian developments which occurred during wartime. See also: POLITICS: Chronological Periods & Elections; SCIENCE.

Colonial Wars

Beers. *The French.* (See 40)

Beers. *The French and the British in the Old Northwest.* (See 132)

American Revolutionary War

Adams. *American Independence.* (See 265)

[230] Gephart, Ronald M. *Periodical Literature on the American Revolution: Historical Research and Changing Interpretations, 1898-1970, a Selective Bibliography.* Washington, D.C.: Library of Congress, 1971. 93 pp. Organized by topic. Index. Not annotated.

[231] Greene, Jack P. *The Reappraisal of the American Revolution in Recent Historical Literature.* (American Historical Association. Service Center for Teachers of History. Publication number 68.) Washington, D.C.: Service Center for Teachers of History, 1967. 82 pp. Interpretive essay. No index. Not annotated.

[232] Morgan, Edmund Sears. *The American Revolution: a Review of Changing Interpretations.* (American Historical Association. Service Center for Teachers of History. Publication number 6.) Washington, D.C.: Service Center for Teachers of History, 1958. 20 pp. Interpretive essay. No index. Not annotated.

[233] U.S. Library of Congress. General Reference and Bibliography Division. *The American Revolution; a Selected Reading List.* Washington, D.C.: G.P.O., 1968. 38 pp. Organized by topic. Index. Not annotated.

Civil War

[234] Beers, Henry Putney. *Guide to the Archives of the Government of the Confederate States of America.* (U.S. National Archives. *Publication,* number 68-15.) Washington, D.C.: G.P.O., 1968. 536 pp. Organized by topic. Index. Annotated.

[235] Bridges, Leonard Hal. *Civil War and Reconstruction.* 2d ed. (American Historical Association. Service Center for Teachers of History. Publication number 5.) Washington, D.C.: Service Center for Teachers of History, 1962. 25 pp. Interpretive essay. No index. Not annotated.

Coulter. *Confederate States.* (See 422)

[236] Crandall, Marjorie Lyle. *Confederate Imprints: A Checklist.* 2 vols. Boston: Boston Atheneum, 1955. Organized by topic. Index. Minority of items annotated.

[237] Donald, David. *The Nation in Crisis, 1861-1877.* New York: Appleton-Century-Crofts, 1969. 92 pp. Organized by topic. Index. Not annotated.

[238] Dornbusch, Charles Emil. *Military Bibliography of the Civil War; Regimental Publications and Personal Narratives.* 2 vols. to date. New York: New York Public Library, 1961-. Organized by state. Index. Not annotated.

[239] Fishwick, Marshall W., and Hollis, William M. *Preliminary Checklist of Writings about R. [Robert] E. Lee.* Charlottesville: Bibliographical Society of the University of Virginia, 1951. 42 pp. Organized by topic. Index. Not annotated.

[240] Harwell, Richard Barksdale. *More Confederate Imprints.* 2 vols. Richmond: Virginia State Library, 1957. Organized by topic. Index. Minority of items annotated.

[241] Kibby, Leo P. *Book Review References for a Decade of Civil War Books, 1950-1960.* San Jose, Calif.: Spartan Bookstore, 1961. 64 pp. Supplement, 1961, 13 pp. Organized alphabetically by author. No index. Not annotated.

[242] May, George S. *Michigan Civil War History: An Annotated Bibliography.* Detroit: Wayne State University, 1961. 128 pp. Organized alphabetically by type of publication. Index. Annotated.

[243] Munden, Kenneth White, and Beers, Henry Putney. *Guide to Federal Archives Relating to the Civil War.* (U.S. National Archives. *Publication,* number 63-1.) Washington, D.C.: G.P.O., 1962. 721 pp. Organized by topic. Index. Annotated.

[244] Nevins, Allan, *et al. Civil War Books, a Critical Bibliography.* 2 vols. Baton Rouge: Louisiana State University, 1967-1969. Organized by topic. Index. Annotated.

[245] O'Quinlivan, Michael, and Gill, Roland P. *An Annotated Bibliography of the United States Marine Corps in the Civil War.* Rev. ed. Washington, D.C.: Marine Corps, 1968. 15 pp. Organized alphabetically by author. No index. Annotated.

[246] Rittenhouse, Jack DeVire. *New Mexico Civil War Bibliography, 1861-1865; an Annotated Checklist of Books and Pamphlets.* Enl. ed. Houston, Tex.: Stagecoach Press, 1961. 36 pp. Organized alphabetically by author. No index. Annotated.

[247] Shetler, Charles. *West Virginia Civil War Literature; an Annotated Bibliography.* Morgantown: West Virginia University, 1963. 184 pp. Organized alphabetically by author. Index. Annotated.

[248] Sinclair, Donald A. *A Bibliography: the Civil War and New Jersey.* New Brunswick, N.J.: Friends of the Rutgers University Library, 1968. 186 pp. Organized by topic. Index. Annotated.

[249] Smith, David Rollin. *The Monitor & the Merrimac: a Bibliography.* Los Angeles: University of California, Los Angeles, 1968. 35 pp. Organized alphabetically by author. No index. Annotated.

[250] U.S. Department of the Army. Army Library. *The Civil War; a Catalog of Books in the Army Library Pertinent to the American Civil War.* 2d centennial ed. Washington, D.C.: G.P.O., 1965. 111 pp. Organized by topic. No index. Not annotated.

[251] U.S. Library of Congress. Map Division. *Civil War Maps, an Annotated List of Maps and Atlases.* Washington, D.C.: G.P.O., 1961. 138 pp. Organized by state. Index. Annotated.

[252] U.S. National Archives. *Civil War Maps in the National Archives.* Washington, D.C.: G.P.O., 1964. 127 pp. Organized by topic. Index. Annotated.

World War I

[253] Hilliard, Jack B. *An Annotated Bibliography of the United States Marine Corps in the First World War.* Washington, D.C.: Marine Corps, 1967. 16 pp. Organized alphabetically by author. No index. Annotated.

[254] *The Two World Wars; a Selective Bibliography.* Oxford, Eng.: Pergamon, 1965. 246 pp. Organized by topic. No index. Annotated.

World War II

Bureau of Railway Economics. *In Defense and War.* (See 227)

California, University of. *Japanese American Evacuation.* (See 369)

Ellinger and Rosinski. *Sea Power.* (See 44)

[255] Morton, Louis. *Writings on World War II.* (American Historical Association. Service Center for Teachers of History. Publication number 66.) Washington, D.C.: Service Center for Teachers of History, 1967. 54 pp. Interpretive essay. No index. Not annotated.

[256] O'Quinlivan, Michael, and Hilliard, Jack B. *An Annotated Bibliography of the United States Marine Corps in the Second World War.* Washington, D.C.: Marine Corps, 1965. 42 pp. Organized by military campaign. Index. Annotated.

The Two World Wars. (See 254)

[257] Ziegler, Janet. *World War II: Books in English, 1945-65.* Stanford, Calif.: Hoover Institution on War, Revolution and Peace, 1971. 223 pp. Organized by topic. Index. Not annotated.

Korean War

[258] Blanchard, Carroll Henry, Jr. *Korean War Bibliography and Maps of Korea.* Albany, N.Y.: Korean Conflict Resolution Foundation, 1964. 181 pp. Organized by topic. No index. Not annotated.

Branches of Armed Services

Includes bibliographies which consider the branches of armed service individually. See also: MILITARY: General & Miscellaneous, and Wars; SCIENCE; ECONOMICS: Transportation.

Air Force

[259] Dornbusch, Charles Emil. *Unit Histories of the United States Air Forces.* Hampton Bays, N.Y.: Hampton Books, 1958. 56 pp. Organized by flight group. No index. Not annotated.

Gibbs-Smith. *Flying.* (See 403)

Higham. *Maritime, Naval and Aeronautical History.* (See 263)

Army

[260] Dornbusch, Charles Emil. *Histories, Personal Narratives: United States Army; a Checklist.* 2d ed. of *Histories of American Army Units, World Wars I and II and Korean Conflict, with some Earlier Histories.* Cornwallville, N.Y.: Hope Farm Press, 1967. 402 pp. Organized by army unit. No index. Minority of items annotated.

Dornbusch. *Military Bibliography of the Civil War.* (See 238)

Marine Corps

[261] Dollen, Charles. *Bibliography of the United States Marine Corps.* New York: Scarecrow, 1963. 115 pp. Organized alphabetically by author. Index. Not annotated.

[262] Hilliard, Jack B. *An Annotated Reading List of United States Marine Corps History.* Washington, D.C.: Marine Corps, 1966. 58 pp. Organized alphabetically by author. Index. Annotated.

Hilliard. *Marine Corps in the First World War.* (See 253)

O'Quinlivan and Gill. *Marine Corps in Civil War.* (See 245)

O'Quinlivan and Hilliard. *Marine Corps in Second World War.* (See 256)

Navy

Albion. *Naval and Maritime History.* (See 91)

Anderson. *Submarines.* (See 401)

Ellinger and Rosinski. *Sea Power.* (See 44)

[263] Higham, Robin D. *An Introduction to Maritime, Naval and Aeronautical History.* Chapel Hill: University of North Carolina Library, 1960. 48 pp. Organized by topic. No index. Not annotated.

Smith. *Monitor & Merrimac.* (See 249)

[264] U.S. Navy Department. Library. *United States Naval History; a Bibliography.* 5th ed. Washington, D.C.: G.P.O., 1969. 34 pp. Organized by topic. No index. Minority of items annotated.

6 / POLITICS

Political Science & Miscellaneous

Includes bibliographies which consider references to political information and to general political activities. Special attention is called to the bibliographies of political science. Many of them include references to other social sciences (e.g., economics, foreign affairs, sociology). See also: ECONOMICS: General & Miscellaneous, and Theories & "Isms"; POLITICS: Groups & Parties; SOCIAL LIFE: General & Miscellaneous.

[265] Adams, Thomas Randolph. *American Independence: the Growth of an Idea, a Bibliographical Study of the American Political Pamphlets Printed between 1764 and 1776 dealing with the Dispute between Great Britain and her Colonies.* Providence, R.I.: Brown University, 1965. 200 pp. Organized by topic. Index. Annotated.

[266] Brock, Clifton. *The Literature of Political Science; a Guide for Students, Librarians, and Teachers.* New York: Bowker, 1969. 232 pp. Organized by topic. Index. Annotated.

Chicago. *Federal-State-Local Relations.* (See 291)

Davis, *et al. Urbanization and Changing Land Use.* (See 56)

Ekirch. *Intellectual History.* (See 444)

Gaines. *Concealed Authorship.* (See 277)

Garrison. *Politics and Elections.* (See 286)

[267] Harmon, Robert Bartlett. *Political Science; a Bibliographical Guide to the Literature.* Metuchen, N.J.: Scarecrow, 1965. 388 pp. Supplement, 1968. Organized by topic. Index. Minority of items annotated.

[268] Holler, Frederick L. *The Information Sources of Political Science.* Santa Barbara, Calif.: ABC-Clio, 1971. 264 pp. Organized by topic. Index. Annotated.

[269] Jonas, Frank H. *Bibliography on Western Politics; Selected Annotated, with Introductory Essays.* Salt Lake City: Institute of Government, University of Utah, 1958. 167 pp. Organized by state. No index. Annotated.

[270] Maryland, University of. Bureau of Governmental Research. *Political Science; a Selected Bibliography of Books in Print, with Annotations.* College Park: Author, 1961. 97 pp. Organized by topic. No index. Annotated.

[271] Nehring, Earl. *Selected Bibliography of Periodical Literature on American Politics, 1940-1958.* Lawrence: University of Kansas, 1958. 62 pp. Organized by topic. No index. Most items annotated.

Sirken. *Life Tables.* (See 390)

U.S. Air Force Academy. Library. *The Congress and America's Future.* (See 306)

U.S. Commission on Intergovernmental Relations. *Intergovernment Relations.* (See 298)

Wasserman. *Statistics Sources.* (See 119)

[272] Wynar, Lubomyr R. *Guide to Reference Materials in Political Science; a Selective Bibliography.* 2 vols. Denver: Colorado Bibliographic Institute, 1966-1968. Organized by topic. Index. Annotated.

Groups & Parties

Includes bibliographies which consider organized political factions, cliques, parties, etc. Also included are groups which tend to support a consistent political point of view regardless of their types of organization. See also: ECONOMICS: Theories & "Isms"; POLITICS: Political Science & Miscellaneous.

Aptheker. *Student Rebellion.* (See 546)

Bassett. *Socialism.* (See 64)

[273] Beck, Carl, and McKechnie, J. Thomas. *Political Elites; a Selected Computerized Bibliography.* Cambridge, Mass.: M.I.T., 1968. 661 pp. Organized by topic with cross references. Index. Not annotated.

[274] Delaney, Robert Finley. *The Literature of Communism in America; a Selected Reference Guide.* Washington, D.C.: Catholic University of America, 1962. 433 pp. Organized by topic. Index. Annotated.

Dunmore. *Poverty, Participation, Protest.* (See 554)

[275] Ellsworth, Ralph Eugene, and Harris, Sara M. *The American Right Wing; a Report to the Fund for the Republic, Inc.* (Graduate School of Library Science. University of Illinois. *Occasional Papers,* number 59.) Urbana: University of Illinois, 1960. 50 pp. Organized by topic. No index. Annotated.

[276] Fund for the Republic. *Bibliography on the Communist Problem in the United States.* New York: Author, 1955. 474 pp. Organized by topic. Index. Annotated.

[277] Gaines, Pierce Welch. *Political Works of Concealed Authorship During the Administration of Washington, Adams, and Jefferson, 1789-1809, with Attributions.* New Haven: Yale University, 1959. 148 pp. Organized by date of publication. Index. Not annotated.

Garrison. *Politics and Elections.* (See 286)

[278] Goldwater, Walter. *Radical Periodicals in America, 1890-1950; a Bibliography with Brief Notes.* New Haven: Yale University, 1964. 51 pp. Organized alphabetically by periodical. No index. Annotated.

Jones and Ripley. *Parties in Congress.* (See 300)

[279] Muller, Robert H., *et al. From Radical Left to Extreme Right: Current Periodicals of Protest, Controversy, or Dissent, with Dispassionate Summaries.* 2d ed. 2 vols. Ann Arbor, Mich.: Campus Publishers, 1970; Metuchen, N.J.: Scarecrow, 1972. Organized by topic. Index. Annotated.

[280] Seidman, Joel Isaac. *Communism in the United States—a Bibliography.* Ithaca, N.Y.: Cornell University, 1969. 526 pp. Organized alphabetically by author. Index. Annotated.

[281] Texas, University of. Tarlton Law Library. *Bibliography on Student Activism, 1963-1970.* Austin: Author, 1970. 84 pp. Organized by type of publication. No index. Not annotated.

Tompkins. *Loyalty-Security Programs.* (See 297)

[282] U.S. Congress. Senate. Committee on Government Operations. *Congressional Investigations of Communism and Subversive Activities; Summary Index, 1918 to 1956.* Washington, D.C.: G.P.O., 1956. 383 pp.

Organized by committees performing investigations. Index. Not annotated.

U.S. Library of Congress. General Reference and Bibliography Division. *Presidents.* (See 12)

[283] Wynar, Lubomyr R. *American Political Parties, a Selective Guide to Parties and Movements of the 20th Century.* Littleton, Colo.: Libraries Unlimited, 1969. 427 pp. Organized by topic. Index. Minority of items annotated.

Chronological Periods & Elections

Includes bibliographies which consider the election process and its results, in general and in specific time periods. See also: MILITARY: Wars; POLITICS: Political Science & Miscellaneous, and Groups & Parties; CHRONOLOGICAL PERIODS.

Adams. *American Independence.* (See 265)

[284] Berwick, Keith B. *The Federal Age, 1789-1829; America in the Process of Becoming.* (American Historical Association. Service Center for Teachers of History. Publication number 40.) Washington, D.C.: Service Center for Teachers of History, 1961. 40 pp. Interpretive essay. No index. Not annotated.

Elkins and McKitrick. *Founding Fathers.* (See 330)

[285] Freidel, Frank Burt. *The New Deal in Historical Perspective.* 2d ed. (American Historical Association. Service Center for Teachers of History. Publication number 25.) Washington, D.C.: Service Center for Teachers of History, 1965. 25 pp. Interpretive essay. No index. Not annotated.

Freitag. *Presidential Inaugurations.* (See 4)

Gaines. *Concealed Authorship.* (See 277)

[286] Garrison, Lloyd W. *American Politics and Elections: Selected Abstracts of Periodical Literature (1964-1968).* Santa Barbara, Calif.: ABC-Clio, 1968. 45 pp. Organized by topic. Author index. Well annotated.

[287] Hicks, John D. *Normalcy and Reaction, 1921-1933; an Age of Disillusionment.* (American Historical Association. Service Center for Teachers of History. Publication number 32.) Washington, D.C.: Service Center for Teachers of History, 1960. 21 pp. Interpretive essay. No index. Not annotated.

[288] Mowry, George E. *The Progressive Era, 1900-1918; Recent Ideas and New Literature.* 2d ed. (American Historical Association. Service Center for Teachers of History. Publication number 10.) Washington, D.C.: Service Center for Teachers of History, 1964. 23 pp. Interpretive essay. No index. Not annotated.

Stewart. *Era of Franklin D. Roosevelt.* (See 576)

[289] Szekely, Kalman S. *Electoral College; a Selective Annotated Bibliography.* Littleton, Colo.: Libraries Unlimited, 1970. 125 pp. Organized by topic. Index. Annotated.

Tompkins. *Vice President.* (See 304)

U.S. Library of Congress. General Reference and Bibliography Division. *Presidents.* (See 12)

Wynar. *Political Parties.* (See 283)

Public Administration

Includes bibliographies which consider bureaucracy, government planning, interagency operations, interlevel operations, and other types of political influence on operation of social institutions. See also: POLITICS: Political Science & Miscellaneous, and Federal Government.

Bollens, *et al. County Government.* (See 217)

[290] California, University of. Bureau of Public Administration. *Conflict of Interest in the Federal Government.* Berkeley: Author, 1961. 66 pp. Organized by topic. No index. Annotated.

California, University of. *Criminal Justice.* (See 327)

California, University of. *Public Employees.* (See 97)

[291] Chicago. Joint Reference Library. *Federal-State-Local Relations, a Selected Bibliography.* Chicago: Library for American Municipal Association and Council of State Governments, 1954. 39 pp. Organized by topic. Index. Not annotated.

[292] Cornell University. Graduate School of Business and Public Administration. *Basic Library in Public Administration.* Ithaca, N.Y.: Author, 1956. 59 pp. Organized alphabetically by author. No index. Not annotated.

Hunt. *Public Utilities.* (See 83)

McDermott and Coleman. *Regulation of Business.* (See 84)

[293] Mars, David, and Frederickson, H. George. *Suggested Library in Public Administration.* With supplements. Los Angeles: University of Southern California, 1964. 203 pp. Organized by topic. Index. Not annotated.

Pittsburgh, University of. *Small Business.* (See 85)

Powell. *Books of a New Nation.* (See 573)

[294] Regional Economic Development Institute. *A Bibliography of Materials in the Field of Regional Economic Development.* Washington, D.C.: Department of Commerce, 1966. 99 pp. Organized by topic. Index. Most items annotated.

[295] Sekler-Hudson, Catheryn. *Bibliography on Public Administration.* Washington, D.C.: American University, 1949. 55 pp. Organized by topic. Index. Annotated.

Silva and Boyd. *Legislative Apportionment.* (See 313)

Social Science Research Council. *Civil-Military Relations.* (See 229)

[296] Tennessee Valley Authority. Library. *Bibliography for the T.V.A. Program.* Unnumbered revision. Knoxville, Tenn.: Author, 1968. 77 pp. Organized by topic. No index. Not annotated.

Tompkins. *Investigation of Lobbying.* (See 302)

[297] Tompkins, Dorothy C. *Loyalty-Security Programs for Federal Employees.* Berkeley: Bureau of Public Administration, University of California, 1955. 69 pp. Organized by topic. No index. Annotated.

Tompkins. *State Governments.* (See 314)

Tompkins. *Vice President.* (See 304)

U.S. Bureau of Land Management. *Public Lands.* (See 63)

[298] U.S. Commission on Intergovernmental Relations. *Intergovernment Relations in the United States; a Selected Bibliography on Interlevel and Interjurisdictional Relations.* Washington, D.C.: G.P.O., 1955. 207 pp. Organized by topic. No index. Not annotated.

U.S. Department of Health, Education and Welfare. *Social Security.* (See 116)

[299] U.S. Department of Health, Education and Welfare. Library. *Grants-in-aid; a Bibliography of Selective References, 1861-1960.* Washington, D.C.: G.P.O., 1962. 91 pp. Organized by topic. Index to legislative material. Annotated.

U.S. Library of Congress. General Reference and Bibliography Division. *Capitol.* (See 307)

U.S. Library of Congress. General Reference and Bibliography Division. *Presidents.* (See 12)

U.S. Library of Congress. General Reference and Bibliography Division. *White House.* (See 308)

Federal Government

Includes bibliographies which consider various agencies, functions, and offices of the federal government. See also: FOREIGN AFFAIRS; ECONOMICS; MILITARY; POLITICS.

California, University of. *Conflict of Interest.* (See 290)

Freitag. *Presidential Inaugurations.* (See 4)

[300] Jones, Charles O., and Ripley, Randall B. *The Role of Political Parties in Congress: a Bibliography and Research Guide.* Tucson: University of Arizona, 1966. 41 pp. Organized by topic. No index. Annotated.

Powell. *Books of a New Nation.* (See 573)

[301] Tompkins, Dorothy C. *Changes in Congress: Proposals to Change Congress, Term of Members of the House; a Bibliography.* Berkeley: Institute of Governmental Studies, University of California, 1966. 43 pp. Organized by topic. Index. Annotated.

[302] Tompkins, Dorothy C. *Congressional Investigation of Lobbying; a Selected Bibliography.* Berkeley: Bureau of Public Administration, University of California, 1956. 32 pp. Organized by topic. No index. Most items annotated.

[303] Tompkins, Dorothy C. *Investigating Procedures of Congressional Committees—a Bibliography.* Berkeley: Bureau of Public Administration, University of California, 1954. 38 pp. Organized by topic. No index. Annotated.

Tompkins. *Loyalty-Security Programs.* (See 297)

[304] Tompkins, Dorothy C. *The Office of Vice President; a Selected Bibliography.* Berkeley: Bureau of Public Administration, University of California, 1957. 19 pp. Organized by topic. No index. Not annotated.

[305] Tompkins, Dorothy C. *Presidential Succession—a Bibliography.* Berkeley: Institute of Governmental Studies, University of California, 1965. 29 pp. Organized by topic. No index. Annotated.

Tompkins. *Supreme Court.* (See 337)

Tompkins. *Wire Tapping.* (See 321)

[306] U.S. Air Force Academy. Library. *The Congress and America's Future.* (*Special Bibliography Series,* number 32.) Washington, D.C.: G.P.O., 1965. 22 pp. Organized by topic. No index. Not annotated.

U.S. Bureau of Land Management. *Public Lands.* (See 63)

U.S. Congress. Senate. Committee on Government Operations. *Investigations of Communism.* (See 282)

U.S. Department of Health, Education and Welfare. *Grants-in-aid.* (See 299)

U.S. Library of Congress. General Reference and Bibliography Division. *Presidents.* (See 12)

[307] U.S. Library of Congress. General Reference and Bibliography Division. *The United States Capitol; a Selected List of References.* Washington, D.C.: G.P.O., 1949. 34 pp. Organized alphabetically by author. Index. Annotated.

[308] U.S. Library of Congress. General Reference and Bibliography Division. *The White House.* Washington, D.C.: G.P.O., 1961. 59 pp. (Supplement to 1939 and 1953 editions.) Organized by topic. Index. Annotated.

State Government

Includes bibliographies which consider various agencies, functions, and offices of state governments. See also: GEOGRAPHY & LOCAL HISTORY: States (by Name).

[309] Boston University. Bureau of Public Administration. *Bibliography on State and Local Government in New England.* Boston: Author, 1952. 233 pp. Organized by topic. No index. Not annotated.

[310] Council of State Governments. *State Government: an Annotated Bibliography.* Chicago: Author, 1959. 46 pp. Organized by topic. No index. Annotated.

[311] Halevy, Balfour J. *Selective Bibliography on State Constitutional Revision.* 2d ed. New York: National Municipal League, 1967. 177 pp. Supplement, 26 pp. Organized by topic. Index. Not annotated.

[312] Pullen, William Russell. *A Check List of Legislative Journals Issued Since 1937 by the States of the United States of America.* Chicago: American Library Association, 1955. 59 pp. Organized by state. No index. Not annotated.

[313] Silva, Ruth C., and Boyd, William J. D. *Selected Bibliography on Legislative Apportionment and Districting.* New York: National Municipal League, 1963. 51 pp. Organized by type of publication. No index. Not annotated.

[314] Tompkins, Dorothy C. *State Governments and Administration; a Bibliography.* Berkeley: Bureau of Public Administration, University of California, 1954. 269 pp. Organized by topic. Index. Not annotated.

[315] U.S. Air Force Academy. Library. *The States and the Urban Crisis.* (*Special Bibliography Series,* number 43.) Washington, D.C.: G.P.O., 1969. 46 pp. Organized by topic. No index. Not annotated.

Constitutional Issues

Includes bibliographies which consider various legal problems arising from interpretations of the constitution. Important issues included are civil liberties, civil rights, and legal aspects of intergroup relations. See also: POLITICS: Political Science & Miscellaneous, and Law & Crime; POPULATION; SOCIAL LIFE: Problems.

Breuer. *Constitutional Development in New York.* (See 182)

[316] Brooks, Alexander D. *Civil Rights and Liberties in the United States, an Annotated Bibliography.* New York: Civil Liberties Educational Foundation, 1962. 151 pp. Organized by topic. No index. Annotated.

[317] McCoy, Ralph Edward. *Freedom of the Press; an Annotated Bibliography.* Carbondale: Southern Illinois University, 1968. Unpaged [approximately 250 pp.]. Organized alphabetically by author. Index. Annotated.

[318] Mooney, Chase Curran. *Civil Rights: Retrospect and Prospects.* (American Historical Association. Service Center for Teachers of History. Publication number 37.) Washington, D.C.: Service Center for

Teachers of History, 1966. 18 pp. Interpretive essay. No index. Not annotated.

Servies. *John Marshall.* (See 19)

Swindler. *Law on Journalism.* (See 510)

[319] Thompson, Edgar T., and Thompson, Alma Macy. *Race and Region; a Descriptive Bibliography Compiled with Special Reference to the Relations between Whites and Negroes in the United States.* Chapel Hill: University of North Carolina, 1949. 194 pp. Organized by topic. Index. Most items annotated.

Tompkins. *Changes in Congress.* (See 301)

[320] Tompkins, Dorothy C. *Confession Issue—from McNab to Miranda, a Bibliography.* Berkeley: Institute of Governmental Studies, University of California, 1968. 100 pp. Organized by topic. Index. Annotated.

Tompkins. *Congressional Committees.* (See 303)

Tompkins. *Presidential Succession.* (See 305)

Tompkins. *Supreme Court.* (See 337)

[321] Tompkins, Dorothy C. *Wire Tapping—a Selected Bibliography.* Berkeley: Bureau of Public Administration, University of California, 1955. 30 pp. Organized by topic. No index. Annotated.

[322] Tuskegee Institute. Department of Records and Research. *A Bibliography of the Student Movement Protesting Segregation and Discrimination, 1960.* Tuskegee, Ala.: Author, 1961. 10 pp. Organized alphabetically by author. No index. Not annotated.

U.S. Special Staff for Employee Management Relations and Equal Employment Opportunities. *Not Just Some of Us.* (See 564)

Williams. *Eight Negro Bibliographies.* (See 364)

Law & Crime

Includes bibliographies which consider constitution making, the legal process, courts, court procedure, crime, crime causation, and law books. See also: POLITICS: Political Science & Miscellaneous, and Constitutional Issues; SOCIAL LIFE: Problems.

Adams. *Burs under the Saddle.* (See 141)

[323] American Bar Association. Committee on Business Law Libraries. *Recommended Law Books.* Chicago: American Bar Association, 1969. 309 pp. Organized by topic. No index. Annotated.

[324] Andrews, Joseph L., *et al. The Law in the United States of America: a Selective Bibliographical Guide.* New York: New York University, 1965. 100 pp. Organized by topic. No index. Annotated.

[325] Becker, Harold K., and Fekenes, George T. *Law Enforcement; a Selected Bibliography.* Metuchen, N.J.: Scarecrow, 1968. 257 pp. Organized by topic. Index. Most items annotated.

Breuer. *Constitutional Development in New York.* (See 182)

[326] Cabot, Phillippe S. De Q. *Juvenile Delinquency: a Critical Annotated Bibliography.* New York: Wilson, 1946. 166 pp. Organized alphabetically by author. Index. Annotated.

California, University of. *Interest of a Child.* (See 518)

[327] California, University of. Bureau of Public Administration. *Administration of Criminal Justice, 1949-1956; a Selected Bibliography.* Sacramento: California State Board of Corrections, 1956. 351 pp. Supplementary to *Sources for the Study of the Administration of Criminal Justice, 1938-1948; a Selected Bibliography.* Organized by topic. Index. Minority of items annotated.

[328] Chambliss, William J., and Seidman, Robert B. *Sociology of the Law: a Research Bibliography.* Berkeley: Glendessary, 1970. 113 pp. Organized by topic. Index. Not annotated.

[329] Dahl, Richard C., and Bolden, C.E. *The American Judge, a Bibliography.* Vienna, Va.: Coiner Publications, 1968. 330 pp. Organized by topic. Index. Not annotated.

Dykes. *Billy the Kid.* (See 13)

[330] Elkins, Stanley M., and McKitrick, Eric. *The Founding Fathers: Young Men of the Revolution.* (American Historical Association. Service Center for Teachers of History. Publication number 44.) Washington, D.C.: Service Center for Teachers of History, 1962. 28 pp. Interpretive essay. No index. Not annotated.

Halevy. *State Constitutional Revision.* (See 311)

Hargrett. *Constitutions of Indians.* (See 378)

Jacobson and Mersky. *Water Law.* (See 72)

Keller. *Alcohol.* (See 557)

[331] McDade, Thomas M. *The Annals of Murder; a Bibliography of Books and Pamphlets on American Murders from Colonial Times to 1900.* Norman: University of Oklahoma, 1961. 360 pp. Organized alphabetically by murderer. Index. Annotated.

[332] Mersky, Roy M. *Law Books for Non-law Libraries and Laymen.* Dobbs Ferry, N.Y.: Oceana, 1969. 110 pp. Organized by topic. Index. Most items annotated.

Meyer. *Urban Crisis.* (See 561)

[333] Pollak, Otto. *Crime Causation; Selected Bibliography of Studies in the United States, 1939-1949.* Philadelphia: University of Pennsylvania, 1950. 53 pp. Organized by topic. No index. Not annotated.

Pullen. *Legislative Journals.* (See 312)

Servies. *John Marshall.* (See 19)

[334] Setaro, Franklyn Christopher. *A Bibliography of the Writings of Roscoe Pound.* Cambridge, Mass.: Harvard University, 1942. 193 pp. Organized by type of publication. Index. Minority of items annotated.

Swindler. *Law on Journalism.* (See 510)

[335] Tompkins, Dorothy C. *Bail in the United States.* Berkeley: Institute of Governmental Studies, University of California, 1964. 49 pp. Organized by topic. Index. Annotated.

Tompkins. *Confession Issue.* (See 320)

[336] Tompkins, Dorothy C. *The Offender; a Bibliography.* Berkeley: Institute of Governmental Studies, University of California, 1963. 268 pp. Organized by topic. Index. Annotated.

[337] Tompkins, Dorothy C. *The Supreme Court of the United States, a Bibliography.* Berkeley: Bureau of Public Administration, University of California, 1959. 217 pp. Organized by topic. Index. Annotated.

[338] Tompkins, Dorothy C. *White Collar Crime–a Bibliography.* Berkeley: Institute of Governmental Studies, University of California, 1967. 85 pp. Organized by topic. Index. Annotated.

Tompkins. *Wire Tapping.* (See 321)

[339] U.S. Library of Congress. Law Library. *Anglo-American Legal Bibliographies, an Annotated Guide.* Washington, D.C.: G.P.O., 1944. 166 pp. Organized alphabetically by author. No index. Most items briefly annotated.

7 / POPULATION

European

Includes bibliographies which consider contributions of European cultural groups and the experience of these groups in American society and culture. See also: FOREIGN AFFAIRS; GEOGRAPHY & LOCAL HISTORY.

Beers. *The French.* (See 40)

Beers. *The French and British in the Old Northwest.* (See 132)

Cogan. *Pioneer Jews of the California Mother Lode.* (See 536)

[340] Cutsumbis, Michael N. *A Bibliographic Guide to Materials on Greeks in the United States, 1890-1968.* New York: Center for Migration Studies, 1970. 100 pp. Organized by type of publication. Index. Minority of items annotated.

[341] Glanz, Rudolf. *The German Jew in America; an Annotated Bibliography including Books, Pamphlets, and Articles of Special Interest.* Cincinnati, Ohio: Hebrew Union College, 1969. 192 pp. Organized by topic. Index. Minority of items annotated.

Hebrew Union College. *Jewish Americana.* (See 537)

Hostetler. *Bibliography on Amish.* (See 544)

Jaffe. *French Literature in American Magazines.* (See 454)

[342] Kolehmainen, John I. *The Finns in America, a Bibliographical Guide to their History.* Hancock, Mich.: Finnish American Historical Library, 1947. 141 pp. Organized by topic. No index. Not annotated.

Larson. *Swedish Commentators.* (See 424)

Levine. *Jewish Bibliography.* (See 538)

[343] Marcus, Jacob Rader. *An Index to Scientific Articles on American Jewish History.* Cincinnati, Ohio: American Jewish Archives, 1971. 240 pp. Organized alphabetically by author. No index. Not annotated.

Parker and Parker. *Local Government in New York During the Dutch Period.* (See 213)

[344] Pochmann, Henry A., and Schultz, Arthur R. *Bibliography of German Culture in America to 1940.* Madison: University of Wisconsin, 1953. 483 pp. Organized alphabetically by author. Index. Not annotated.

[345] Rischin, Moses. *An Inventory of American Jewish History.* Cambridge, Mass.: Harvard University, 1954. 66 pp. Organized by topic. Index. Annotated.

Stern. *California Jewish History.* (See 162)

[346] Velikonja, Joseph. *Italians in the United States (Bibliography).* Carbondale: Department of Geography, Southern Illinois University, 1963. 90 pp. Organized by topic. Index. Not annotated.

Black (Negro, Afro-American)

Includes bibliographies which consider the experiences and the contributions of Blacks to American society. Slavery and antislavery are included. See also: ECONOMICS: Labor, and Private Wealth & Poverty; POLITICS: Constitutional Issues, and Law & Crime; SOCIAL LIFE.

[347] Bibliography Committee of the New Jersey Library Association. *New Jersey and the Negro; a Bibliography, 1715-1966.* Trenton: Author, 1967. 196 pp. Organized by topic. Index. Annotated.

Bolner. *Racial Imbalance in Public Schools.* (See 548)

[348] California State College, Fresno. Library. *Afro- and Mexican-Americana.* Fresno: Author, 1969. 109 pp. Organized by topic. Index. Not annotated.

[349] Deodene, Frank, and French, William P. *Black American Fiction Since 1952; a Preliminary Checklist.* Chatham, N.J.: Chatham Bookseller, 1970. 25 pp. Organized alphabetically by author. No index. Minority of items annotated.

[350] Dumond, Dwight Lowell. *A Bibliography of Antislavery in America.* Ann Arbor: University of Michigan, 1961. 119 pp. Organized alphabetically by author. No index. Not annotated.

Dunmore. *Poverty, Participation, Protest.* (See 554)

[351] Harlan, Louis R. *The Negro in American History.* (American Historical Association. Service Center for Teachers of History. Publication number 61.) Washington, D.C.: Service Center for Teachers of History, 1965. 29 pp. Interpretive essay. No index. Not annotated.

Hatch. *Black Image.* (See 491)

[352] Jahn, Janheinz. *A Bibliography of Neo-African Literature from Africa, America, and the Caribbean.* New York: Praeger, 1965. 359 pp. Organized by place of publication. Index. Not annotated.

Lawrenz. *Negro Music.* (See 494)

[353] McPherson, James M., *et al. Blacks in America: Bibliographical Essays.* New York: Doubleday, 1971. 430 pp. Organized by topic. Index. Well annotated.

[354] Miller, Elizabeth W. *The Negro in America: a Bibliography.* 2d ed., rev. and enl. Cambridge, Mass.: Harvard University, 1970. 351 pp. Organized by topic. Index. Annotated.

[355] National Urban League. *Selected Bibliography on the Negro.* 4th ed. New York: Author, 1951. 124 pp. Organized by topic. No index. Most items annotated.

[356] Porter, Dorothy. *The Negro in the United States: a Selected Bibliography.* Washington, D.C.: Library of Congress, 1970. 313 pp. Organized by topic. Index. Not annotated.

[357] Porter, Dorothy. *North American Negro Poets; a Bibliographical Checklist of their Writings, 1760-1944.* Hattiesburg, Miss.: Book Farm, 1945. 90 pp. Organized alphabetically by author. No index. Not annotated.

[358] San Fernando Valley State College. *The Black Experience in the United States; a Bibliography . . . .* Los Angeles: Author, 1970. 162 pp. Organized by topic. Index. Not annotated.

Searcher. *Lincoln Today.* (See 18)

Thompson. *The Plantation.* (See 75)

Thompson and Thompson. *Race and Region.* (See 319)

[359] Thompson, Lawrence S. *The Southern Black: Slave and Free: a Bibliography of Anti- and Pro-Slavery Books and Pamphlets and of Social and Economic Conditions in Southern States From the Beginnings to 1950.* Troy, N.Y.: Whitston, 1970. 576 pp. Organized alphabetically by author. No index. Not annotated.

[360] Treworgy, Mildred L., and Foreman, Paul B. *Negroes in the United States; a Bibliography of Materials for Schools.* University Park: Pennsylvania State University, 1967. 93 pp. Organized by topic. Index. Not annotated.

[361] Turner, Darwin T. *Afro-American Writers.* New York: Appleton-Century-Crofts, 1970. 117 pp. Organized by topic. Index. Not annotated.

Tuskegee Institute. *Student Movement.* (See 322)

[362] Washington State Library, Olympia. *The Negro in the State of Washington, 1788-1967; a Bibliography.* Olympia: Author, 1968. 14 pp. Organized by type of publication. No index. Annotated.

Weinberg. *School Integration.* (See 565)

[363] Welsch, Erwin K. *The Negro in the United States; a Research Guide.* Bloomington: Indiana University, 1965. 142 pp. Organized by topic. Index. Annotated.

Whiteman. *Fiction by Negroes.* (See 463)

[364] Williams, Daniel T. *Eight Negro Bibliographies.* New York: Kraus Reprint, 1970. Various pagings. Most of the eight bibliographies are organized by topic. None has an index. None is annotated.

Spanish-Speaking (Chicano, Puerto Rican, etc.)

Includes bibliographies which consider the experiences and the contributions of Spanish-speaking people to American society. See also: ECONOMICS: Labor, and Private Wealth & Poverty; GEOGRAPHY & LOCAL HISTORY: Sections, States (by Name), Parts of States (by Name), and Parts of States (General); POLITICS: Constitutional Issues, and Law & Crime; SOCIAL LIFE: Problems.

[365] Barrios, Ernie. *Bibliografía de Aztlán: an Annotated Chicano Bibliography.* San Diego: Centro de Estudios Chicanos, San Diego State College, 1971. 157 pp. Organized by topic. Index. Annotated.

California State College, Fresno. *Afro- and Mexican-Americana.* (See 348)

Cumberland. *U.S.-Mexican Border.* (See 148)

[366] Nogales, Luis G. *The Mexican American; a Selected and Annotated Bibliography.* 2d ed. Stanford: Stanford University, 1971. 162 pp. Organized alphabetically by author. Index. Annotated.

Potter. *Health and Illness in New Mexico.* (See 563)

Saunders. *Cultural Relations in New Mexico.* (See 181)

[367] Schramko, Linda Fowler. *Chicano Bibliography: Selected Materials on Americans of Mexican Descent.* Sacramento, Calif.: Sacramento State College Library, 1970. 124 pp. Organized by topic. Index. Not annotated.

[368] U.S. Inter-Agency Committee on Mexican American Affairs. *A Guide to Materials Relating to Persons of Mexican Heritage in the United States.* Washington, D.C.: G.P.O., 1969. 184 pp. Organized by type of publication. No index. Not annotated.

Oriental (Asian-American, Chinese, Japanese, etc.)

Includes bibliographies which consider the experiences and the contributions of Orientals to American society. See also: FOREIGN AFFAIRS; GEOGRAPHY & LOCAL HISTORY: States (by Name), Parts of States (by Name), and Parts of States (General); SOCIAL LIFE: Problems.

[369] California, University of. Library. *Japanese American Evacuation and Resettlement, Catalog of Material in the the General Library.* Berkeley: Author, 1958. 177 pp. Organized by type of publication. No index. Not annotated.

[370] Fujimoto, Isao, *et al. Asians in America; a Selected Annotated Bibliography.* Davis: Department of Applied Behavioral Sciences, University of California, Davis, 1971. 295 pp. Organized by topic. Index. Annotated.

[371] Hansen, Gladys C., and Heintz, William F. *The Chinese in California; a Brief Bibliographic History.* Portland, Ore.: Richard Abel, 1970. 140 pp. Organized alphabetically by author. Index. Annotated.

[372] Hennefrund, Helen E., and Cummings, Orpha. . . . *Bibliography on the Japanese in American Agriculture.* (U.S. Department of Agriculture. *Bibliographical Bulletin,* number 3.) Washington, D.C.: G.P.O., 1943. 61 pp. Organized alphabetically by author. Index. Annotated.

Liu. *Americans and Chinese.* (See 46)

[373] Nimura, Taku Frank. *Japanese in the United States; a Bibliography.* Sacramento, Calif.: Sacramento State College Library, 1969. 26 pp. Organized alphabetically by author. No index. Annotated.

Rubano. *Culture and Behavior in Hawaii.* (See 168)

American Indian

Includes bibliographies which consider Indian culture and Indian relation to Anglo-American society. See also: ECONOMICS: Private Wealth & Poverty; GEOGRAPHY & LOCAL HISTORY: Sections, and States (by Name); SOCIAL LIFE: Problems.

[374] Bean, Lowell John, and Lawton, Harry W. *A Bibliography of the Cahuilla Indians of California.* Banning, Calif.: Malki Museum, 1967. 28 pp. Organized alphabetically by author. No index. Not annotated.

Beers. *The French and British in the Old Northwest.* (See 132)

[375] Edwards, Everett E., and Rasmussen, Wayne D. *A Bibliography on the Agriculture of the American Indians.* (U.S. Department of Agriculture. *Miscellaneous Publications,* number 447.) Washington, D.C.: G.P.O., 1942. 107 pp. Organized by topic. Index. Annotated.

[376] Fenton, William N., *et al. American Indian and White Relations to 1830, Needs & Opportunities for Study; an Essay.* Chapel Hill: University of North Carolina, 1957. 138 pp. Organized by type of publication. Index. Annotated.

[377] Hagan, William T. *The Indian in American History.* (American Historical Association. Service Center for Teachers of History. Publication number 50.) New York: Service Center for Teachers of History, 1963. 26 pp. Interpretive essay. No index. Not annotated.

[378] Hargrett, Lester. *A Bibliography of the Constitutions and Laws of the American Indians.* Cambridge, Mass.: Harvard University, 1947. 124 pp. Organized by Indian nation. Index. Annotated.

Haywood, *Folklore and Folksong.* (See 451)

[379] Martin, F. Ellen. *Bibliography: the Navajo Indians.* Tempe: Arizona State University, 1968. 39 pp. Organized alphabetically by author. No index. Not annotated.

[380] Minnesota Historical Society. *Chippewa and Dakota Indians: a Subject Catalog of Books, Pamphlets, Periodical Articles and Manuscripts.* St. Paul: Author, 1969. 131 pp. Organized by topic. No index. Not annotated.

[381] Murdock, George Peter. *Ethnographic Bibliography of North America.* 3d ed. New Haven, Conn.: Human Relations Area Files, 1960. 393 pp. Organized by topic. Index. Not annotated.

Potter. *Health and Illness in New Mexico.* (See 563)

Saunders. *Cultural Relations in New Mexico.* (See 181)

[382] Snodgrass, Marjory P. *Economic Development of American Indians and Eskimos, 1930-1967; a Bibliography.* (U.S. Department of the Interior. *Bibliography Series,* number 10.) Washington, D.C.: G.P.O., 1968. 263 pp. Organized by topic. Index. Not annotated.

[383] Tyler, Samuel Lyman. *The Ute People; a Bibliographical Checklist.* Provo, Utah: Brigham Young University, 1964. 120 pp. Organized by type of publication. No index. Not annotated.

[384] U.S. Library of Congress. General Reference and Bibliography Division. *Folklore of the North American Indians; an Annotated Bibliography.* Washington, D.C.: G.P.O., 1969. 126 pp. Organized by topic. Index. Annotated.

Migration

Includes bibliographies which consider the movements of people into and out of the United States. Also included are internal migration patterns. See also: ECONOMICS: Agriculture and Labor; POPULATION.

Bailey. *Genealogical and Biographical Sources.* (See 1)

Banks. *Migration of Farm People.* (See 67)

[385] George Washington University. *A Report on World Population Migrations as Related to the United States of America.* Washington, D.C.: Author, 1956. 449 pp. Organized by topic. No index. Annotated.

[386] Lancour, Harold, and Wolfe, Richard J. *A Bibliography of Ship Passenger Lists, 1538-1825.* 3d ed. New York: New York Public Library, 1963. 137 pp. Organized by topic. Index. Annotated.

[387] Mangalam, J.J. *Human Migration; a Guide to Migration Literature in English, 1955-1962.* Lexington: University of Kentucky, 1968. 194 pp. Organized alphabetically by author. Index. Some items annotated.

[388] Scott, Franklin Daniel. *Emigration and Immigration.* 2d ed. (American Historical Association. Service Center for Teachers of History. Publication number 51.) New York: Service Center for Teachers of History, 1966. 63 pp. Interpretive essay. No index. Not annotated.

U.S. Department of Agriculture. *Farm Migration.* (See 111)

U.S. National Agricultural Library. *Migratory Labor.* (See 112)

[389] Wilber, George L., and Bang, James S. *Internal Migration in the United States, 1940-1957; a List of References.* State College: Mississippi State University, 1958. 52 pp. Organized by topic. No index. Not annotated.

Vital Statistics

Includes bibliographies which consider statistical data specifically related to population and demographic characteristics of American society. See also: ECONOMICS: Private Wealth & Poverty, and Statistics; SOCIAL LIFE: Problems.

[390] Sirken, Monroe G., *et al. Guide to United States Life Tables, 1900-1959.* Washington, D.C.: Department of Health, Education and Welfare, 1963. 63 pp. Organized by topic. No index. Not annotated.

[391] U.S. Library of Congress. Census Library Project. *Catalog of United States Census Publications 1790-1945.* Reprint of 1950 ed. New York: Greenwood, 1968. 320 pp. Organized by topic. Index. Annotated.

[392] U.S. Library of Congress. Census Library Project. *State Censuses; an Annotated Bibliography of Censuses of Population Taken after the Year 1790 by States and Territories of the United States.* Reprint of 1948 ed. New York: B. Franklin, 1969. 73 pp. Organized alphabetically by state. No index. Annotated.

U.S. Office of Health Statistics Analysis. *Vital Statistics.* (See 399)

8 / SCIENCE

General & Miscellaneous

Includes bibliographies which consider general and miscellaneous scientific activities and their relation to American society.

[393] Bell, Whitfield, Jr. *Early American Science, Needs and Opportunities for Study.* Williamsburg, Va.: Institute of Early American History and Culture, 1955. 85 pp. Organized by topic. Index. Most items annotated.

[394] California, University of. Los Alamos Scientific Laboratory. *Some Ethical and Social Problems of Science and Technology: a Bibliography of the Literature from 1955.* Los Alamos, N.M.: Author, 1964. 58 pp. Organized alphabetically by author. No index. Not annotated.

Petsche. *Salvage Archeology.* (See 123)

Medicine

Includes bibliographies which consider biology, physical ailments, psychological problems, and general health conditions. See also: SOCIAL LIFE: Problems.

Bahr. *Disaffiliated Man.* (See 547)

[395] Blake, John Ballard, and Roos, Charles. *Medical Reference Works, 1679-1966; a Selected Bibliography.* Chicago: Medical Library Association, 1967. 343 pp. Organized by topic. Index. Most items annotated.

Faberow. *Suicide Prevention.* (See 555)

[396] Guerra, Francisco. *American Medical Bibliography, 1639-1783.* New York: Harper, 1962. 885 pp. Organized by type of publication. Index. Annotated.

Hays. *David Starr Jordan.* (See 475)

Keller. *Alchohol.* (See 557)

[397] Miller, Genevieve. *Bibliography of the History of Medicine in the United States and Canada, 1939-1960.* Baltimore: The Johns Hopkins University, 1964. 428 pp. Organized by topic. Index. Not Annotated.

Potter. *Health and Illness in New Mexico.* (See 563)

[398] U.S. National Library of Medicine. *Early American Medical Imprints; a Guide to Works Printed in the United States, 1668-1820.* Washington, D.C.: G.P.O., 1961. 240 pp. Organized alphabetically by author. Index. Minority of items annotated.

[399] U.S. Office of Health Statistics Analysis. *Annotated Bibliography on Vital and Health Statistics.* Rockville, Md.: G.P.O., 1970. 143 pp. Organized by topic. Index. Annotated.

[400] U.S. Veterans Administration. Medical and General Reference Library. *Medical Care of the Veteran in the United States, 1870-1960.* Washington, D.C.: G.P.O., 1963. 106 pp. Organized by date of publication. Index. Not annotated.

Technology

Includes bibliographies which consider the application of science to economic activity. Includes invention and physical science activities (physics, chemistry). See also: ECONOMICS: Industry & Mining, and Transportation; MILITARY: General & Miscellaneous.

Albion. *Naval and Maritime History.* (See 91)

[401] Anderson, Frank J. *Submarines, Submariners, Submarining, a Checklist of Submarine Books in the English Language, Principally of the Twentieth Century.* Hamden, Conn.: Shoestring, 1963. 40 pp. Organized alphabetically by author. Index. Not annotated.

[402] Ferguson, Eugene S. *Bibliography of the History of Technology.* Cambridge, Mass.: Society for the History of Technology and M.I.T., 1968. 347 pp. Organized by topic. Index. Annotated.

[403] Gibbs-Smith, Charles H. *The History of Flying.* Cambridge, Eng.: National Book League, 1957. 32 pp. Organized by topic. Index. Annotated.

Higham. *Maritime, Naval and Aeronautical History.* (See 263)

[404] Hindle, Brooke. *Technology in Early America: Needs and Opportunities for Study.* Chapel Hill: University of North Carolina, 1966. 145 pp. Organized by topic. Index. Annotated.

[405] Michigan State University of Agriculture and Applied Science, East Lansing. Labor and Industrial Relations Center. *Economic and Social Implications of Automation.* 3 vols. East Lansing: Author, 1960-1966. Organized by topic. Index. Annotated.

Munn. *Coal Industry.* (See 88)

[406] Ordway, Frederich I. *Annotated Bibliography of Space Science and Technology with an Astronomical Supplement. A History of Astronautical Book Literature—1931 through 1961.* 3d ed. Washington, D.C.: Arfor, 1962. 77 pp. Organized by date of publication. Index. Annotated.

Renstrom. *Wilbur and Orville Wright.* (See 23)

Swanson. *Oil and Gas.* (See 89)

Thompson. *Railroads before 1841.* (See 95)

U.S. Administration on Aging. *Words on Aging.* (See 527)

U.S. Navy Department. Library. *Naval History.* (See 264)

[407] U.S. Library of Congress. Division of Aeronautics. *Aeronautic Americana; a Bibliography of Books and Pamphlets on Aeronautics Published in America Before 1900.* New York: Institute of the Aeronautical Sciences, 1943. 40 pp. Organized by date of publication. Index. Annotated.

[408] U.S. Library of Congress. General Reference and Bibliography Division. *The Social Impact of Science: a Select Bibliography with a Section on Atomic Power.* Washington, D.C.: G.P.O., 1945. 51 pp. Organized by type of publication. No index. Minority of items annotated.

[409] Weiss, John H. *Technology and Social History.* Cambridge, Mass.: Harvard University Program on Technology and Society, 1971. 93 pp. Organized by topic. Index. Annotated.

[410] Whitehill, Walter Muir, *et al. The Arts in Early American History: Needs and Opportunities for Study.* Chapel Hill, N.C.: Institute of Early American History and Culture, 1965. 170 pp. Organized by topic. Index. Annotated.

[411] Wroth, Lawrence C. *Some American Contributions to the Art of Navigation, 1519-1802.* Providence, R.I.: Friends of the John Carter Brown Library, 1947. 41 pp. Organized by date of publication. No index. Annotated.

9 / INTELLECTUAL & CULTURAL LIFE

Education

Includes bibliographies which consider schools of all levels and types; libraries; social problems relating to education (e.g., religion in public schools, racial and ethnic integration of students in public schools). Includes student activities (e.g., student political activism). See also: ECONOMICS: Theories & "Isms"; INTELLECTUAL & CULTURAL LIFE: Literature, Poetry, & Philosophy, and Authors; SOCIAL LIFE: Problems.

Aptheker. *Student Rebellion.* (See 546)

[412] Bailyn, Bernard. *Education in the Forming of American Society; Needs and Opportunities for Study.* Chapel Hill: University of North Carolina, 1960. 147 pp. Organized by topic. Index. Annotated.

Bolner. *Racial Imbalance in Public Schools.* (See 548)

Booth, *et al. Culturally Disadvantaged.* (See 549)

[413] Bronson, Barbara. *Bibliographical Guides to the History of American Libraries.* (Graduate School of Library Science. University of Illinois. *Occasional Papers,* number 32.) Urbana: University of Illinois, 1953. 11 pp. Organized by topic. No index. Annotated.

California. *Farm Migrant Education.* (See 551)

Crabbs and Holmquist. *Higher Education and World Affairs.* (See 552)

Drouin. *The School Question.* (See 553)

[414] Harris, Michael G. *A Guide to Research in American Library History.* Metuchen, N.J.: Scarecrow, 1968. 186 pp. Organized by topic. Index. Annotated.

Hays. *David Starr Jordan.* (See 475)

King. *Horace Mann.* (See 477)

Little. *Religion and Public Education.* (See 558)

[415] Park, Joe. *The Rise of American Education; an Annotated Bibliography.* Evanston, Ill.: Northwestern University, 1965. 216 pp. Organized by topic. No index. Annotated.

Preminger. *Harry D. Gideonse.* (See 473)

[416] Rarig, Emory W., Jr. *The Community Junior College; an Annotated Bibliography.* New York: Teachers College, 1966. 114 pp. Organized by topic. Index. Annotated.

Skeel and Carpenter. *Noah Webster.* (See 480)

[417] Songe, Alice. *Vocational Education: an Annotated Bibliography of Selected References, 1917-1966 (Below College).* Washington, D.C.: U.S. Department of Health, Education and Welfare. Organized by type of publication. Index. Annotated.

Texas, University of. *Student Activism.* (See 281)

Thomas. *John Dewey.* (See 468)

[418] U.S. Office of Education. *The College Presidency, 1900-1960; an Annotated Bibliography.* (*Bulletin, 1961,* number 9.) Washington, D.C.: G.P.O., 1961. 143 pp. Organized by topic. Index. Annotated.

Weinberg. *School Integration.* (See 565)

Exploration & Travel

Includes bibliographies which consider travel throughout the United States and the exploration of North America by Europeans. Includes personal experiences on trips, descriptions of geographic sites visited, and social conditions witnessed. See also: PERSONAL ACCOUNTS; GEOGRAPHY & LOCAL HISTORY: Sections and States (by Name); ECONOMICS: Transportation; SOCIAL LIFE.

Beers. *The French* (See 40)

[419] Carson, Jane. *Travelers in Tidewater Virginia, 1700-1800; a Bibliography.* Charlottesville: University of Virginia, 1965. 121 pp. Organized by author. Index. Well annotated.

[420] Clark, Thomas D. *Travels in the New South, a Bibliography.* 2 vols. Norman: University of Oklahoma, 1962. Organized chronologically. Index. Well annotated.

[421] Clark, Thomas D. *Travels in the Old South, a Bibliography.* 3 vols. Norman: University of Oklahoma, 1956-1959. Organized chronologically. Index. Well annotated.

[422] Coulter, Ellis Merton. *Travels in the Confederate States, a Bibliography.* Norman: University of Oklahoma, 1961. 289 pp. Organized alphabetically by author. Index. Annotated.

[423] Hubach, Robert Rogers. *Early Midwestern Travel Narratives; an Annotated Bibliography, 1634-1850.* Detroit: Wayne State University, 1961. 149 pp. Organized by date of publication. Index. Annotated.

Lancour and Wolfe. *Passenger Lists.* (See 386)

[424] Larson, Esther Elisabeth. *Swedish Commentators on America, 1638-1865.* New York: New York Public Library, 1963. 139 pp. Organized alphabetically by author. Index. Minority of items annotated.

[425] Monahan, Frank. *French Travelers in the United States, 1765-1932; a Bibliography . . . with Supplement. . . .* Reprint with supplement. New York: Antiquarian Press, 1961. 130 pp. Organized alphabetically by author. Index. Some items annotated.

U.S. Library of Congress. General Reference and Bibliography Division. *Columbus.* (See 14)

[426] U.S. Library of Congress. Map Division. *Maps Showing Explorers' Routes, Trails & Early Roads in the United States: an Annotated List.* Washington, D.C.: G.P.O., 1962. 137 pp. Organized by cartographer. Index. Annotated.

U.S. Library of Congress. Map Division. *Treasure Maps.* (See 125)

U.S. Navy Department. Library. *Naval History.* (See 264)

[427] Wagner, Henry Raup. *The Plains and the Rockies; a Bibliography of Original Narratives . . . 1800-1865.* 3d rev. ed. Columbus, Ohio:

Long's College Book, 1953. 601 pp. Organized by date of publication. Index. Annotated.

[428] Washburne, Wilcomb E. *The Age of Discovery.* (American Historical Association. Service Center for Teachers of History. Publication number 63.) Washington, D.C.: Service Center for Teachers of History, 1966. 26 pp. Interpretive essay. No index. Not annotated.

Wheat. *Gold Rush.* (See 205)

Wroth. *Art of Navigation.* (See 411)

Fine Arts & Architecture

Includes bibliographies which consider painting, sculpture, building design and construction, and illustrations. See also: SCIENCE: Technology; INTELLECTUAL & CULTURAL LIFE: Literature, Poetry, & Philosophy, and Authors.

[429] Chamberlin, Mary Wells. *Guide to Art Reference Books.* Chicago: American Library Association, 1959. 418 pp. Organized by topic. Index. Annotated.

[430] Foster, Donald L. *Check List of U.S. Government Publications in the Arts.* (Graduate School of Library Science. University of Illinois. *Miscellaneous Papers,* number 96.) Urbana: University of Illinois, 1969. 48 pp. Organized by topic. Index. Not annotated.

[431] Hitchcock, Henry Russell. *American Architectural Books; a List of Books, Portfolios, and Pamphlets on Architecture and Related Subjects, Published in America before 1895.* "New Printing with new preface and additional material." Minneapolis: University of Minnesota, 1962. 130 pp. Organized alphabetically by author. Index. Minority of items annotated.

[432] Lucas, E. Louise. *Art Books; a Basic Bibliography on the Fine Arts.* Greenwich, Conn.: New York Graphic Society, 1968. 245 pp. Organized by topic. Index. Not annotated.

[433] The New York Historical Society. *Dictionary of Artists in America, 1564-1860.* New York: Yale University, 1957. 759 pp. Organized alphabetically by artist. No index. Not annotated.

[434] Princeton University. Library. *Early American Book Illustrators and Wood Engravers, 1670-1870. . . .* 2 vols. Princeton: Author, 1968. Organized alphabetically by artist. No index. Annotated.

[435] Roos, Frank J. *Bibliography of Early American Architecture Constructed before 1860 in Eastern and Central United States.* Rev. and annot. Urbana: University of Illinois, 1968. 389 pp. Organized by sections of the United States. Index. Minority of items annotated.

Whitehill. *Arts in Early American History.* (See 410)

Literature, Poetry, & Philosophy

Includes bibliographies which consider fiction, nonfiction, poetry, and folklore and legend. Included are bibliographies of philosophic speculation and general intellectual history. *Not included* are bibliographies of specific and individual writers of fiction, nonfiction, or poetry. See also: ECONOMICS: Theories and "Isms"; POLITICS: Political Science & Miscellaneous; POPULATION: Black; INTELLECTUAL & CULTURAL LIFE: Authors.

[436] Altick, Richard Daniel, and Wright, Andrew. *Selective Bibliography for the Study of English and American Literature.* 4th ed. New York: Macmillan, 1971. 164 pp. Organized by topic. Well indexed. Not annotated.

[437] American Studies Association. Committee on Microfilm Bibliography. *Bibliography of American Culture, 1493-1875.* Ann Arbor, Mich.: University Microfilm, 1957. 228 pp. Organized by topic. No index. Not annotated.

[438] Blanck, Jacob Nathaniel. *Bibliography of American Literature.* 5 vols. to date. New Haven: Yale University, 1955-. Organized alphabetically by author. No index. Annotated.

Boger. *Southern Mountaineer.* (See 137)

Bremner. *Social History Since 1860.* (See 512)

[439] Clark, Harry Hayden. *American Literature: Poe Through Garland.* New York: Appleton-Century-Crofts, 1971. 148 pp. Organized by topic. Index. Not annotated.

[440] Coan, Otis Welton, and Lillard, Richard G. *America in Fiction.* 5th ed. Palo Alto, Calif.: Pacific Books, 1967. 232 pp. Organized by topic. Index. Annotated.

[441] Davidson, Lavette J. *A Guide to American Folklore.* Denver, Colo.: Sage Books, 1951. 132 pp. Organized by source of information. No index. Not annotated.

[442] Davis, Richard Beale. *American Literature Through Bryant, 1585-1830.* New York: Appleton-Century-Crofts, 1969. 135 pp. Organized by topic. Index. Not annotated.

Deodene and French. *Black Fiction.* (See 349)

Dobie. *Southwest.* (See 149)

Drake. *Almanacs.* (See 506)

Dykes. *Billy the Kid.* (See 13)

[443] Eicheberger, Clayton L. *A Guide to Critical Reviews of United States Fiction, 1870-1910.* Metuchen, N.J.: Scarecrow, 1971. 415 pp. Organized alphabetically by author. Index. Not annotated.

[444] Ekirch, Arthur A., Jr. *American Intellectual History.* 2d ed. (American Historical Association. Service Center for Teachers of History. Publication number 53.) Washington, D.C.: Service Center for Teachers of History, 1967. 33 pp. Interpretive essay. No index. Not annotated.

Gaines. *Concealed Authorship.* (See 277)

[445] Gerstenberger, Donna Lorine, and Hendrick, George. *The American Novel; a Checklist of Twentieth Century Criticism on Novels Written Since 1789.* 2 vols. Denver, Colo.: Alan Swallow, 1961-1970. Organized alphabetically by author. No index. Not annotated.

[446] Gohdes, Clarence Louis Frank. *Bibliographical Guide to the Study of the Literature of the U.S.A.* 3d ed., rev. and enl. Durham, N.C.: Duke University, 1970. 134 pp. Organized by topic. Index. Most items annotated.

[447] Gohdes, Clarence Louis Frank. *Literature and Theater of the States and Regions of the U.S.A.* Durham, N.C.: Duke University, 1967. 276 pp. Organized by states. No index. Not annotated.

Grob. *Social History before 1860.* (See 513)

[448] Grolier Club, New York. *One Hundred Influential American Books Printed before 1900.* New York: Author, 1947. 139 pp. Organized chronologically by date of publication. Index. Annotated.

[449] Hackett, Alice Payne. *70 Years of Best Sellers, 1895-1965.* New York: Bowker, 1967. 280 pp. Organized chronologically. Index. Not annotated.

[450] Havlice, Patricia Pate. *Index to American Author Bibliographies.* Metuchen, N.J.: Scarecrow, 1971. 204 pp. Organized alphabetically by author. Index. Not annotated.

[451] Haywood, Charles. *A Bibliography of North American Folklore and Folksong.* 2d rev. ed. 2 vols. New York: Dover, 1961. Well organized by topic. Index. Minority of items annotated.

[452] Holman, C. Hugh. *The American Novel through Henry James.* New York: Appleton-Century-Crofts, 1966. 102 pp. Organized by topic. Index. Not annotated.

[453] Irish, Wynot R. *The Modern American Muse; a Complete Bibliography of American Verse, 1900-1925.* Syracuse, N.Y.: Syracuse University, 1950. 259 pp. Organized by date of publication. No index. Not annotated.

[454] Jaffe, Adrian H. *Bibliography of French Literature in American Magazines of the 18th Century.* East Lansing: Michigan State University, 1951. 27 pp. Organized by date of publication. Index. Annotated.

[455] Jones, Howard Mumford, and Ludwig, Richard M. *Guide to American Literature and its Backgrounds Since 1890.* 3d ed., rev. and enl. Cambridge, Mass.: Harvard University, 1964. 240 pp. Organized by topic. Index. Annotated.

[456] Leary, Lewis Gaston. *Articles on American Literature, 1900-1950.* Durham, N.C.: Duke University, 1954. 437 pp. Supplement, 1968. Organized by topic. No index. Not annotated.

Lomax and Cowell. *Folksong and Folklore.* (See 496)

[457] Modern Language Association of America. General Topics VI. *Literature and Society, 1950-1955.* Coral Gables, Fla.: University of Miami, 1956. 57 pp. Supplements, 1962, 71 pp.; 1967, 160 pp. Organization varies between original and supplementary volumes. Index. Annotated.

[458] Nilon, Charles H. *Bibliography of Bibliographies in American Literature.* New York: Bowker, 1970. 483 pp. Organized by topic. Index. Not annotated.

[459] Pennsylvania, University of. Library. *Check List of Poetry by American Authors Published in the English Colonies of North America and the United States through 1865. . . .* Philadelphia: Author, 1951. 63 pp. Organized alphabetically by author. No index. Not annotated.

Porter. *Negro Poets.* (See 357)

[460] Rubin, Louis Decimus, Jr. *A Bibliographical Guide to the Study of Southern Literature.* Baton Rouge: Louisiana State University, 1969. 351 pp. Organized by topic. No index. Annotated.

[461] Spiller, Robert, *et al. Literary History of the United States: Bibliography.* 2 vols. Comprising vol. II of *Literary History of the United States.* 3d ed. rev. New York: Macmillan, 1963. 268 pp. Organized by topic. Index. Annotated.

Turner. *Afro-American Writers.* (See 361)

U.S. Library of Congress. General Reference and Bibliography Division. *Folklore of Indians.* (See 384)

[462] U.S. Library of Congress. General Reference and Bibliography Division. *Sixty American Poets, 1896-1944.* Rev. ed. Washington, D.C.: G.P.O., 1954. 155 pp. Organized by poet. No index. Not annotated.

[463] Whiteman, Maxwell. *A Century of Fiction by American Negroes, 1853-1952; a Descriptive Bibliography.* Philadelphia: n.p., 1955. 64 pp. Organized alphabetically by author. No index. Most items annotated.

[464] Wright, Lyle Henry. *American Fiction, 1774-1850; a Contribution toward a Bibliography.* 2d rev. ed. San Marino, Calif.: Henry E. Huntington Library and Art Gallery, 1969. 355 pp. Organized alphabetically by author. Index. Not annotated.

[465] Wright, Lyle Henry. *American Fiction, 1851-1875; a Contribution toward a Bibliography. Additions and Corrections Appended.* San Marino, Calif.: Henry E. Huntington Library and Art Gallery, 1965. 438 pp. Organized alphabetically by author. Index. Not annotated.

[466] Wright, Lyle Henry. *American Fiction, 1876-1900; a Contribution toward a Bibliography.* San Marino, Calif.: Henry E. Huntington Library and Art Gallery, 1966. 683 pp. Organized alphabetically by author. Index. Not annotated.

Authors (Nonfiction & Poets)

Includes bibliographies which consider *only* nonfiction writers (e.g., economists, philosophers, educators, journalists). Writers of fiction are included if they also wrote a significant amount of nonfiction commentaries on American society. Arranged alphabetically by biographical name (see titles). *Living* authors and poets are *excluded.* See also: ECONOMICS: Theories and "Isms"; POLITICS: Political Science & Miscellaneous; INTELLECTUAL & CULTURAL LIFE: Literature, Poetry, & Philosophy.

[467] Johnson, Oakley C., and Reeve, Carl. *Writings By and About Daniel De Leon; a Bibliography.* New York: American Institute for Marxist

Studies, 1966. 26 pp. Organized alphabetically by author. No index. Most items annotated.

[468] Thomas, Milton Halsey. *John Dewey; a Centennial Bibliography.* Chicago: University of Chicago, 1962. 370 pp. Organized by date of publication and alphabetically by author. Index. Not annotated.

McVicker. *J. Frank Dobie.* (See 146)

[469] Ferguson, Alfred Riggs. *The Merrill Checklist of Ralph Waldo Emerson.* Columbus, Ohio: Charles E. Merrill, 1970. 44 pp. Organized by type of publication. No index. Not annotated.

[470] Sowder, William J. *Emerson's Reviewers and Commentators; a Biographical and Bibliographical Analysis of . . . Periodical Criticism.* Hartford, Conn.: Transcendental Books, 1968. 64 pp. Organized by type of publication. Index. Annotated.

[471] Fisher, Irving Norton. *A Bibliography of the Writings of Irving Fisher.* New Haven: Yale University, 1961. 543 pp. Organized by date of publication. Index. Not annotated.

[472] Marsh, Philip Merrill. *Freneau's Published Prose: a Bibliography.* Metuchen, N.J.: Scarecrow, 1970. 167 pp. Organized by date of publication. No index. Not annotated.

[473] Preminger, Alexander S., *et al. Urban Educator: Harry D. Gideonse, Brooklyn College and the City University of New York.* New York: Twayne, 1970. 304 pp. Organized by date of publication. Index. Annotated.

[474] Stein, Gordon. *Robert G. Ingersoll; a Checklist.* Kent, Ohio: Kent State University, 1969. 128 pp. Organized by type of publication. Index. Not annotated.

[475] Hays, Alice Newman. *David Starr Jordan; a Bibliography of his Writings, 1871-1931.* Stanford, Calif.: Stanford University, 1952. 195 pp. Organized by topic. Index. Not annotated.

[476] Woodbridge, Hensley Charles, *et al. Jack London; a Bibliography.* Georgetown, Calif.: Talisman, 1966. 422 pp. Organized by type of publication. Index. Minority of items annotated.

[477] King, Clyde S. *Horace Mann, 1796-1859; a Bibliography.* Dobbs Ferry, N.Y.: Oceana, 1966. 453 pp. Organized by type of publication. Index. Minority of items annotated.

[478] Enoch Pratt Free Library, Baltimore. *H.L.M.; The Mencken Bibliography.* Baltimore: The Johns Hopkins University, 1961. 367 pp. Organized by type of work. Index. Minority of items annotated.

[479] Nolite, William Henry. *The Merrill Checklist of H.L. Mencken.* Columbus, Ohio: Charles E. Merrill, 1969. 30 pp. Organized by type of publication. No index. Not annotated.

Setaro. *Roscoe Pound.* (See 334)

[480] Skeel, Emily Ellsworth, and Carpenter, Edwin H., Jr. *A Bibliography of the Writings of Noah Webster.* New York: New York Public Library, 1958. 655 pp. Organized by type of publication. Index. Annotated.

[481] Kansas State Teachers College, Emporia. *A Bibliography of William Allen White.* 2 vols. Emporia: Author, 1962. Organized by type of publication. Index. Some items annotated.

[482] Tanner, James T. F. *Walt Whitman; a Supplementary Bibliography, 1961-1967.* Kent, Ohio: Kent State University, 1968. 59 pp. Organized alphabetically by author. No index. Not annotated.

[483] U.S. Library of Congress. Reference Department. *Walt Whitman; a Catalog based upon the collection of the Library of Congress.* Washington, D.C.: G.P.O., 1955. 147 pp. Organized by type of publication. Index. Minority of items annotated.

[484] White, William. *Walt Whitman's Journalism; a Bibliography.* Detroit: Wayne State University, 1969. 73 pp. Organized by date of publication. No index. Not annotated.

[485] Ramsey, Richard David. *Edmund Wilson; a Bibliography.* New York: David Lewis, 1971. 345 pp. Organized by type of publication. No index. Minority of items annotated.

Turnbull. *Woodrow Wilson.* (See 22)

Theater, Speech, & Music

Includes bibliographies which consider theater and dramatic arts; speech, forensics, and speech patterns; and music (classical, folk, jazz, and popular). See also: POPULATION: Black; INTELLECTUAL & CULTURAL LIFE: Literature, Poetry, & Philosophy.

[486] Bergquist, G. William. *Three Centuries of English and American Plays, a Checklist, England: 1500-1800, United States: 1714-1830.* New York: Hafner, 1963. 281 pp. Organized alphabetically by author. No index. Not annotated.

[487] Brockett, Oscar G., *et al.* *A Bibliographical Guide to Research in Speech and Dramatic Art.* Chicago: Scott, Foresman, 1963. 118 pp. Organized by topic. No index. Annotated.

[488] Coffin, Tristram. *The British Traditional Ballad in North America.* Rev. ed. Philadelphia: American Folklore Society, 1963. 186 pp. Organized by topic. Index. Well annotated.

[489] Duckles, Vincent Harris. *Music Reference and Research Materials; an Annotated Bibliography.* 2d ed. New York: Free Press, 1967. 385 pp. Organized by topic. Index. Annotated.

[490] Edmunds, John, and Boelzner, Gordon. *Some Twentieth Century American Composers; a Selective List.* 2 vols. New York: New York Public Library, 1959-1960. Organized alphabetically by composer. Index. Not annotated.

Gohdes. *Literature and Theater.* (See 447)

[491] Hatch, James Vernon. *Black Image on the American Stage: a Bibliography of Plays and Musicals, 1770-1970.* New York: D.B.S. Publications, 1970. 162 pp. Organized chronologically. Index. Not annotated.

[492] Hudson, E. Long. *American Drama from Its Beginnings to the Present.* New York: Appleton-Century-Crofts, 1970. 78 pp. Organized by topic. Index. Not annotated.

[493] Kennington, Donald. *The Literature of Jazz; a Critical Guide.* Chicago: American Library Association, 1971. 142 pp. Organized by topic. Index. Annotated.

[494] Lawrenz, Marguerite Martha. *Bibliography and Index of Negro Music.* Detroit: Board of Education, 1968. 52 pp. Organized by topic. Index. Not annotated.

[495] Laws, G. Malcolm, Jr. *Native American Balladry; a Descriptive Study and Bibliographical Syllabus.* Rev. ed. Philadelphia: American Folklore Society, 1964. 298 pp. Organized by topic. Index. Annotated.

[496] Lomax, Alan, and Cowell, Sidney Robertson. *American Folksong and Folklore, a Regional Bibliography.* New York: Service Center of the Progressive Education Association, 1942. 59 pp. Organized by topic. No index. Annotated.

[497] McMillan, James B. *Annotated Bibliography of Southern American Speech.* Coral Gables, Fla.: University of Miami, 1971. 173 pp. Organized by topic. Index. Minority of items annotated.

[498] Merriam, Alan P., and Benford, Robert J. *A Bibliography of Jazz.* Philadelphia: American Folklore Society, 1954. 145 pp. Organized alphabetically by author. Index. Not annotated.

[499] Pennsylvania, University of. Library. *Check List of American Drama Published in the English Colonies of North America and the United States through 1865. . . .* Philadelphia: Author, 1951. 92 pp. Organized alphabetically by author. Index. Not annotated.

[500] Reisner, Robert George. *The Literature of Jazz; a Selective Bibliography.* 2d ed. New York: New York Public Library, 1959. 63 pp. Organized alphabetically by author. No index. Not annotated.

[501] Stratman, Carl Joseph. *American Theatrical Periodicals, 1798-1967; a Bibliographical Guide.* Durham, N.C.: Duke University, 1970. 133 pp. Organized by date of publication. Index. Annotated.

[502] Stratman, Carl Joseph. *Bibliography of the American Theater, Excluding New York City.* Chicago: Loyola University, 1965. 397 pp. Organized alphabetically by state. Index. Minority of items annotated.

Communications Media

Includes bibliographies which consider journalism (newspaper, magazine, and periodical), almanacs, and issues relating to communications media (e.g., freedom of the press). Includes electric communications media (e.g., telephone, radio, and television). See also: ECONOMICS: Theories & "Isms"; POLITICS: Constitutional Issues and Law & Crime; INTELLECTUAL & CULTURAL LIFE: Literature, Poetry, & Philosophy.

[503] Bear, James A., Jr., and Bear, Mary Caperton. *A Checklist of Virginia Almanacs, 1732-1850.* Charlottesville: Bibliographical Society of the University of Virginia, 1962. 250 pp. Organized by date of publication. Index. Not annotated.

[504] Brigham, Clarence Saunders. *History and Bibliography of American Newspapers, 1690-1820.* 2 vols. Worcester, Mass.: American Antiquarian Society, 1947. Supplement, *Additions and Corrections to History and Bibliography of American Newspapers, 1961.* 50 pp. Organized by state. Index. Annotated.

[505] Brown, Charles Henry. *Reader's Guide to the Literature of Journalism; a Selected Annotated Bibliography for the General Reader and Student.* University Park: Pennsylvania State University, 1961. 87 pp. Organized by topic. No index. Annotated.

[506] Drake, Milton. *Almanacs of the United States.* 2 vols. New York: Scarecrow. 1962. Organized by state in which almanac was published. No index. Not annotated.

Enoch Pratt Library. *H.L.M.* [Mencken] (See 478)

Goldwater. *Radical Periodicals.* (See 278)

[507] Hansen, Donald A., and Parsons, J. Herschell. *Mass Communications: a Research Bibliography.* Santa Barbara, Calif.: Glendessary, 1968. 144 pp. Organized by topic. Index. Not annotated.

Jaffe. *French Literature in American Magazines.* (See 454)

Kansas State Teachers College. *William Allen White.* (See 481)

McCoy. *Freedom of Press.* (See 317)

Muller, *et al. Left to Right.* (See 279)

Nolite. *Mencken.* (See 479)

[508] Price, Warren C. *The Literature of Journalism, an Annotated Bibliography.* Minneapolis: University of Minnesota, 1959. 489 pp. Supplement: Price, Warren C., and Pickett, Calder M. *An Annotated Journalism Bibliography, 1958-1968.* 1970. 285 pp. Organized by topic (supplement: alphabetically by author). Index. Annotated.

[509] Rose, Oscar. *Radio Broadcasting and Television, an Annotated Bibliography.* New York: H.H. Wilson, 1947. 120 pp. Organized by topic. Index. Annotated.

[510] Swindler, William F. *A Bibliography of Law on Journalism.* New York: Columbia University, 1947. 190 pp. Organized by topic. Index. Annotated.

White. *Whitman's Journalism.* (See 484)

[511] Wolseley, Roland Edgar. *The Journalist's Bookshelf; an Annotated & Selected Bibliography of United States Journalism.* 7th ed. Philadelphia: Chilton, 1961. 225 pp. Organized by topic. Index. Annotated.

10 / SOCIAL LIFE

General & Miscellaneous

Includes bibliographies which consider general American social life and sporting activities. See also: INTELLECTUAL & CULTURAL LIFE: Literature, Poetry, & Philosophy, and Authors; SOCIAL LIFE: Problems.

American Studies Association. *American Culture.* (See 437)

[512] Bremner, Robert H. *American Social History Since 1860.* New York: Appleton-Century-Crofts, 1971. 126 pp. Organized by topic. Index. Not annotated.

Glenn, *et al. Social Stratification.* (See 556)

[513] Grob, Gerald N. *American Social History before 1860.* New York: Appleton-Century-Crofts, 1970. 137 pp. Organized by topic. Index. Not annotated.

[514] Henderson, Robert William. *Early American Sports; a Check-List of Books by American and Foreign Authors Published in America Prior to 1860 Including Sporting Songs.* 2d ed., rev. and enl. New York: A.S. Barnes, 1953. 234 pp. Organized alphabetically by author. Index. Most items annotated by descriptive titles.

Modern Language Association. *Literature.* (See 457)

[515] Murdoch, Joseph S. *The Library of Golf, 1743-1966; a Bibliography of Golf Books, Indexed Alphabetically, Chronologically, & by Subject.* Detroit: Gale Research, 1968. 314 pp. Organized alphabetically by author. Index. Most items annotated.

Wasserman. *Statistics Sources.* (See 119)

Women & Family

Includes bibliographies which consider women's life styles, marriage, home activities (e.g., cooking), problems of youth, and geriatrics. See also: SOCIAL LIFE: General & Miscellaneous, and Problems.

[516] Aldous, Joan, and Hill, Reuben. *International Bibliography of Research in Marriage and the Family, 1900-1964.* Minneapolis: University of Minnesota, 1967. 508 pp. Organized by key word in context and by topic. Well indexed. Not annotated.

Booth, *et al. Culturally Disadvantaged.* (See 549)

[517] Brown, Eleanor Parker, and Brown, Bob. *Culinary Americana; Cookbooks Published . . . from 1860 through 1960.* New York: Roving Eye, 1961. 417 pp. Organized by place of publication. Index. Not annotated.

Cabot. *Juvenile Delinquency.* (See 326)

[518] California, University of. Bureau of Public Administration. *In the Interest of a Child.* Sacramento: California State Board of Corrections, 1959. 251 pp. Organized by topic. Index. Annotated.

[519] Chambers, Merritt M., and Exton, Elaine. *Youth—Key to America's Future; an Annotated Bibliography.* Washington, D.C.: American Council on Education, 1949. 117 pp. Organized by topic. Index. Annotated.

[520] Leonard, Eugenia Andrus, *et al. The American Woman in Colonial and Revolutionary Times, 1561-1800.* Philadelphia: University of Pennsylvania, 1962. 169 pp. Organized by topic. No index. Not annotated.

[521] Lincoln, Waldo. *American Cookery Books, 1742-1860.* Rev. and enl. Worcester, Mass.: American Antiquarian Society, 1954. 136 pp. Organized by date of publication. Index. Not annotated.

[522] Ludlow, William L. *A Syllabus and Bibliography of Marriage and the Family.* Rev. and exp. New Concord, Ohio: Radcliffe, 1951. 309 pp. Organized by topic. No index. Not annotated.

[523] Morlock, Maud. *Homemaker Services, History and Bibliography.* Washington, D.C.: Children's Bureau, 1964. 116 pp. Organized by topic. Index. Annotated.

[524] North Carolina, University of. Women's College, Greensboro. Library. *The Women's Collection; a Bibliography of Material on all Matters Pertaining to Women's Interests. . . .* 2 vols. Greensboro: Author, 1944-1950. Supplements, 1950-1955. Organized by topic. Index. Annotated.

[525] Sloane, William. *Children's Books in England & America in the Seventeenth Century.* New York: Columbia University, 1955. 251 pp. Organized by date of publication. Index. Annotated.

[526] Smith, Elsdon Coles. *Personal Names; a Bibliography.* New York: New York Public Library, 1952. 226 pp. Organized by topic. Index. Annotated.

[527] U.S. Administration on Aging. *Words on Aging; a Bibliography.* Washington, D.C.: G.P.O., 1970. 190 pp. Supplement, 1971, 107 pp. Organized by topic. Index. Annotated.

U.S. Department of Agriculture. *Levels of Living.* (See 76)

U.S. Department of Health, Education and Welfare. *Social Security.* (See 116)

U.S. Office of Health Statistics Analysis. *Vital Statistics.* (See 399)

U.S. Social Security Administration. *Poverty in the Sixties.* (See 118)

Religion (General)

Includes bibliographies which consider general religious topics; general religious commentaries and philosophies; and social implications of religion in American life. Because of the predominance of Protestantism in American life, bibliographies cited emphasize Protestant sects and varieties of Christianity, although they also consider other forms of the Judaic-Christian tradition. See also: POPULATION; SOCIAL LIFE: Religion (Groups) and Problems.

[528] Berkowitz, Morris I., and Johnson, J. Edmund. *Social Scientific Studies of Religion: a Bibliography.* Pittsburgh: University of Pittsburgh, 1967. 258 pp. Organized by topic. Index. Not annotated.

[529] Burr, Nelson R. *A Critical Bibliography of Religion in American Life.* 2 vols. Comprising vol. IV of *Religion in America* by James Ward Smith and Leland Jamison. 4 vols. Princeton: Princeton University, 1961. Organized by topic. Index. Well annotated.

[530] Burr, Nelson R. *Religion in American Life.* New York: Appleton-Century-Crofts, 1971. 171 pp. Organized by topic. Index. Not annotated.

Drouin. *School Question.* (See 553)

[531] Gaustad, Edwin Scott. *American Religious History.* (American Historical Association. Service Center for Teachers of History. Publication number 65.) Washington, D.C.: Service Center for Teachers of History, 1966. 27 pp. Interpretive essay. No index. Not annotated.

Hills. *Bible in America.* (See 543)

Little. *Religion and Education.* (See 558)

Stein. *Robert G. Ingersoll.* (See 474)

Williams. *Eight Negro Bibliographies.* (See 364)

Religion (Groups)

Includes bibliographies which consider Catholicism, Judaism, and Protestantism. See also: POPULATION; SOCIAL LIFE: Religion (General).

Catholicism

[532] Ellis, John Tracy. *A Guide to American Catholic History.* Milwaukee, Wis.: Bruce, 1959. 147 pp. Organized by topic. Index. Annotated.

[533] Ellis, John Tracy. *A Select Bibliography of the History of the Catholic Church in the United States.* New York: Declan X. McMullen, 1947. 96 pp. Organized by date and by type of publication. Index. Minority of items annotated.

[534] Vollmar, Edward R. *The Catholic Church in America; an Historical Bibliography.* 2d ed. New York: Scarecrow, 1963. 399 pp. Organized alphabetically by author. Index. Minority of items annotated.

[535] Weber, Francis J. *A Selected Guide to California Catholic History.* Los Angeles: Westernlore, 1966. 227 pp. Organized by type of publication. Index. Some items annotated.

Judaism

[536] Cogan, Sara G. *Pioneer Jews of the California Mother Lode, 1849-1880; an Annotated Bibliography.* Berkeley: Western Jewish History Center, 1968. 54 pp. Organized by type of publication. Index. Annotated.

Glanz. *German Jew in America.* (See 341)

[537] Hebrew Union College-Jewish Institute of Religion. Library. *Jewish Americana . . . to 1850; a Supplement to A. S. W. Rosenbach, an American Jewish Bibliography.* Cincinnati, Ohio: American Jewish Archives, 1954. 114 pp. Organized alphabetically by author. Index. Annotated.

[538] Levine, Allan E. *An American Jewish Bibliography; a List of Books and Pamphlets by Jews or Relating to them Printed in the United States from 1851-1875.* Cincinnati, Ohio: Hebrew Union College-Jewish Institute of Religion, 1959. 100 pp. Organized by date of publication. Index. Minority of items annotated.

Marcus. *American Jewish History.* (See 343)

Rischin. *American Jewish History.* (See 345)

Stern. *California Jewish History.* (See 162)

Protestantism: Bibliographies Which Emphasize Individual Sects, Denominations, Movements.

[539] Brigham Young University. Division of Religion. *A Practical Bibliography of Works on Mormonism.* Provo, Utah: Author, 1944. 19 pp. Organized by topic. No index. Not annotated.

[540] Ehlert, Arnold D. *Brethren Writers, a Checklist. . . .* Grand Rapids, Mich.: Baker Book House, 1969. 83 pp. Poorly organized by topic. No index. Not annotated.

[541] Erie County, New York. Buffalo and Erie County Public Library. *Shaker Literature in the Rare Book Room of the Buffalo and Erie County Public Library.* Rev. ed. Buffalo: Author, 1967. 43 pp. Organized alphabetically by author. No index. Not annotated.

[542] Harrison, Ira E. *A Selected Annotated Bibliography on Store-Front Churches and Other Religious Writings.* Syracuse, N.Y.: Youth Development Center, Syracuse University, 1963. 29 pp. Organized by type of publication. No index. Annotated.

[543] Hills, Margaret T. *The English Bible in America; a Bibliography of Editions of the Bible and the New Testament Published in America, 1777-1957.* New York: American Bible Society, 1961. 477 pp. Organized by date of publication. Index. Annotated.

[544] Hostetler, John A. *Annotated Bibliography on the Amish.* Scottdale, Pa.: Mennonite Publishing, 1951. 100 pp. Organized by type of publication. Index. Annotated.

Kirkpatrick. *Utah and Latter-day Saints.* (See 197)

[545] Starr, Edward C. *A Baptist Bibliography; Being a Registry of Printed Material by and About Baptists.* 16 vols. to date. Rochester, N.Y.: American Baptist Historical Society, 1947-. Organized alphabetically by author. Index. Not annotated.

Problems

Includes bibliographies which consider social problems, issues, and crises. Some problems are integrally related to economic and political problems. Problems include: behavior which does not fit into social norms, mental health problems, social class relationships, minority group problems, poverty problems, social theories, etc. See also: ECONOMICS: Theories & "Isms," Private Wealth & Poverty; POLITICS: Political Science & Miscellaneous, Groups & Parties, and Law & Crime.

Anderson. *Rural Sociology.* (See 66)

[546] Aptheker, Bettina. *Higher Education and the Student Rebellion in the United States, 1960-1969—a Bibliography.* New York: American Institute for Marxist Studies, 1969. 50 pp. Organized by type of publication. Index. Minority of items annotated.

[547] Bahr, Howard M. *Disaffiliated Man; Essays and Bibliography on Skid Row, Vagrancy, and Outsiders.* Toronto, Ont.: University of Toronto, 1970. 428 pp. Organized by topic. Index. Annotated.

[548] Bolner, James. *Racial Imbalance in Public Schools; a Basic Annotated Bibliography.* Baton Rouge: Institute of Government Research, Louisiana State University, 1968. 73 pp. Organized alphabetically by author. Index. Annotated.

[549] Booth, Robert Edmond, *et al. Culturally Disadvantaged; a Bibliography and Keyword-out-of-context (KWOC) Index.* Detroit: Wayne State University, 1967. 803 pp. Organized by topic. Index. Not annotated.

[550] Bracket, Vivianne, *et al. Social Stratification and Poverty: a Selected and Annotated Bibliography.* Madison: University of Wisconsin, 1967. 148 pp. Organized by topic. Index. Annotated.

[551] California Department of Education. *Bibliography on Farm Migrant Education.* Sacramento: Author, 1969. 21 pp. Organized by state. No index. Minority of items annotated.

Chambliss and Seidman. *Sociology of the Law.* (See 328)

[552] Crabbs, Richard F., and Holmquist, Frank W. *United States Higher Education and World Affairs.* New York: Praeger, 1967. 207 pp. Organized by topic. Index. Some items annotated.

Davis, *et al. Urbanization and Changing Land Use.* (See 56)

[553] Drouin, Edmund Gabriel. *The School Question; a Bibliography on Church-State Relations in American Education, 1940-1960.* Washington, D.C.: Catholic University of America, 1963. 261 pp. Organized by topic. Index. Minority of items annotated.

[554] Dunmore, Charlotte. *Poverty, Participation, Protest, Power, and Black America; a Bibliography for Use in Work Education.* New York: Council on Social Work Education, 1970. 67 pp. Organized alphabetically by author. No index. Annotated.

[555] Faberow, Norman L. *Bibliography on Suicide and Suicide Prevention, 1897-1957, 1958-1967.* Chevy Chase, Md.: National Institute of Mental Health, 1969. 203 pp. Organized alphabetically by author. Index. Not annotated.

[556] Glenn, Norval D., *et al. Social Stratification: a Research Bibliography.* Berkeley: Glendessary, 1970. 466 pp. Organized by topic. Index. Not annotated.

Harrison. *Store-Front Churches.* (See 542)

Institute of Labor and Industrial Relations. *Minority Group Employment.* (See 99)

Institute for Rural America. *Poverty.* (See 113)

[557] Keller, Mark. *International Bibliography of Studies on Alcohol.* 2 vols. New Brunswick, N.J.: Rutgers University, 1966-1968. Organized by date of publication. Index. Not annotated.

[558] Little, Lawrence Calvin. *Religion and Public Education; a Bibliography.* 3d ed., rev. and enl. Pittsburgh: University of Pittsburgh Bookstore, 1968. 214 pp. Organized by type of publication. No index. Not annotated.

[559] Mack, Raymond W., *et al. Social Mobility, Thirty Years of Research and Theory; an Annotated Bibliography.* Syracuse, N.Y.: Syracuse University, 1957. 31 pp. Organized alphabetically by author. No index. Annotated.

Manny. *Rural Community Organization.* (See 73)

[560] Messner, Stephen D. *Minority Groups and Housing; a Selected Bibliography, 1950-1967.* Storrs: Center for Real Estate and Urban Economic Studies, University of Connecticut, 1968. 60 pp. Organized by topic. Index. Not annotated.

[561] Meyer, Jon K. *Bibliography on Urban Crisis; Behavioral, Psychological, and Sociological Aspects of Urban Crisis.* Chevy Chase, Md.: National Institute of Mental Health, 1969. 452 pp. Organized by topic. Index. Not annotated.

[562] National Opinion Research Center. *NORC Social Research, 1941-1964; an Inventory of Studies and Publications in Social Research.* Chicago: University of Chicago, 1964. 80 pp. Supplement. Organized by topic. Index. Annotated.

Payne and Bailey. *The Community.* (See 221)

Pollak. *Crime Causation.* (See 333)

[563] Potter, Helen Rose. *Social and Economic Dimensions of Health and Illness Behavior in New Mexico: an Annotated Bibliography.* Albuquerque: University of New Mexico, 1969. 220 pp. Organized by topic. Index. Annotated.

Rubano. *Culture and Behavior in Hawaii.* (See 168)

Schlesinger. *Poverty.* (See 114)

Snodgrass. *Indians and Eskimos.* (See 382)

Thompson and Thompson. *Race and Region.* (See 319)

Tompkins. *Poverty During the Sixties.* (See 115)

Tuskegee Institute. *Student Movement.* (See 322)

U.S. Administration on Aging. *Words on Aging.* (See 527)

U.S. Air Force Academy. Library. *The States and the Urban Crisis.* (See 315)

U.S. Department of Health, Education and Welfare. *Social Security.* (See 116)

U.S. Library of Congress. General Reference and Bibliography Division. *Social Impact of Science.* (See 408)

U.S. Social Security Administration. *Poverty in the Sixties.* (See 118)

[564] U.S. Special Staff for Employee Management Relations and Equal Employment Opportunities. *Not Just Some of Us; a Limited Bibliography on Minority Group Relations.* 2d ed. Baltimore: G.P.O., 1969. 42 pp. Organized by topic. No index. Minority of items annotated.

[565] Weinberg, Meyer. *School Integration; a Comprehensive Classified Bibliography of 3,100 References.* Chicago: Integrated Education Associates, 1967. 137 pp. Organized by topic. Index. Not annotated.

Weiss. *Technology and Social History.* (See 409)

11 / CHRONOLOGICAL PERIODS

Through 1788

Includes bibliographies which consider many social, political, and economic topics, but are limited to (or greatly emphasize) the years before the inauguration of George Washington as president. Bibliographies included here are of such broad topics that they are not classifiable under topics previously listed. See also: POLITICS: Chronological Periods & Elections.

Gephart. *Periodical Literature on the Revolution.* (See 230)

[566] Greene, Evarts Boutell, and Morris, Richard B. *A Guide to the Principal Sources for Early American History (1600-1800) in the City of New York.* 2d ed. New York: Columbia University, 1953. 400 pp. Organized by topic. Index. Annotated.

[567] Greene, Jack P., and Papenfuse, Edward C., Jr. *The American Colonies in the Eighteenth Century, 1689-1763.* New York: Appleton-Century-Crofts, 1969. 132 pp. Organized by topic. Index. Not annotated.

[568] Institute of Early American History and Culture. *Books about Early America: a Selection for Non-professional Readers.* Williamsburg, Va.: Institute of Early American History and Culture, 1965. 48 pp. Organized by topic. Index. Not annotated.

Morgan. *American Revolution.* (See 232)

Powell. *Books of a New Nation.* (See 573)

U.S. Library of Congress. Reference and Bibliography Division. *American Revolution.* (See 233)

[569] Vaughan, Alden T. *The American Colonies in the Seventeenth Century.* New York: Appleton-Century-Crofts, 1971. 147 pp. Organized by topic. Index. Not annotated.

Wheat and Brun. *Maps and Charts before 1800.* (See 130)

[570] Wright, Louis B. *New Interpretations of American Colonial History.* 2d ed. (American Historical Association. Service Center for Teachers of History. Publication number 16.) New York: Service Center for Teachers of History, 1963. 25 pp. Interpretive essay. No index. Not annotated.

1789-1876

Includes bibliographies which consider many social, political, and economic topics, but are limited to (or greatly emphasize) the years between the inauguration of Washington and the election of Rutherford B. Hayes as president. Bibliographies included here are of such broad topics that they are not classifiable under topics above. See also: POLITICS: Chronological Periods & Elections.

Bridges. *Civil War and Reconstruction.* (See 235)

[571] Carman, Harry James, and Thompson, Arthur W. *A Guide to the Principal Sources for American Civilization, 1800-1900, in the City of New York: Printed Materials.* New York: Columbia University, 1962. 630 pp. Organized by topic. Index. Not annotated.

Donald. *Nation in Crisis.* (See 237)

[572] Fehrenbacher, Don E. *Manifest Destiny and the Coming of the Civil War, 1840-1860.* New York: Appleton-Century-Crofts, 1970. 127 pp. Organized by topic. Index. Not annotated.

Garrison. *U.S., 1865-1900.* (See 574)

Greene and Morris. *Early American History.* (See 566)

Institute of Early American History and Culture. *Early America.* (See 568)

Kibby. *Civil War Books, 1950-1960.* (See 241)

Nevins. *Civil War Books.* (See 244)

[573] Powell, John Henry. *The Books of a New Nation: United States Government Publications, 1774-1814.* Philadelphia: University of Pennsylvania, 1957. 170 pp. Organized by topic. Index. Annotated.

U.S. Department of the Army. *Civil War.* (See 250)

Wheat and Brun. *Maps and Charts Before 1800.* (See 130)

1877-1945

Includes bibliographies which consider many social, political, and economic topics, but are limited to (or greatly emphasize) the years between the inauguration of Rutherford B. Hayes as president and the end of World War II. Bibliographies included here are of such broad topics that they are not classifiable under topics above. See also: POLITICS: Chronological Periods & Elections.

Carman and Thompson. *Principal Sources.* (See 571)

[574] Garrison, Curtis Wiswell. *The United States, 1865-1900; a Survey of Current Literature with Abstracts of Unpublished Dissertations.* 3 vols. Fremont, Ohio: Rutherford B. Hayes-Lucy Webb Hayes Foundation, 1943-1945. Organized by topic. Index. Well annotated.

[575] Link, Arthur S., and Leary, William M., Jr. *The Progressive Era and the Great War, 1896-1920.* New York: Appleton-Century-Crofts, 1969. 85 pp. Organized by topic. Index. Not annotated.

Mowry. *The Progressive Era.* (See 288)

National Opinion Research Center. *Social Research.* (See 562)

[576] Stewart, William James. *The Era of Franklin D. Roosevelt: a Selective Bibliography of Periodical and Dissertation Literature, 1945-1966.* Hyde Park, N.Y.: U.S. National Archives and Records Service, 1967. 175 pp. Organized by topic. No index. Annotated.

Ziegler. *World War II.* (See 257)

1945 to Present

Includes bibliographies which consider many social, political, and economic topics, but are limited to (or greatly emphasize) the years since the end of World War II. Bibliographies included here are of such broad topics that they are not classifiable under topics above. See also: POLITICS: Chronological Periods & Elections.

[577] Grantham, Dewey W., Jr. *The United States since 1945.* (American Historical Association. Service Center for Teachers of History. Publication number 71.) Washington, D.C.: Service Center for Teachers of History, 1968. 45 pp. Interpretive essay. No index. Not annotated.

National Opinion Research Center. *Social Research.* (See 562)

Part II

General References

BASIC REFERENCES

The reference works listed here are most useful to the neophyte researcher. They discuss the use and the value of the most popular research tools. The researcher who has had little experience working with specialized information sources will benefit from them. Most of the sources listed in these volumes are included elsewhere in this guide. However, the descriptions in the works cited below are of such value the beginner may wish to consult these reference works to insure that he is properly conducting his research.

Galin, Saul, and Spielberg, Peter. *Reference Books: How to Select and Use Them.* New York: Random House, 1969. 312 pp. A useful compilation which explains the utility of popular reference books. The few major reference books considered are well discussed.

Katz, William A. *Introduction to Reference Work.* 2 vols. New York: McGraw-Hill, 1969. Volume I, subtitled *Basic Information Sources,* is particularly valuable. However, if the researcher has already been introduced to many of the basic works, he may find the essay-length descriptions tedious and of little use.

Winchell, Constance M. *Guide to Reference Books.* 8th ed. Chicago: American Library Association, 1967. 741 pp. Supplements, 1968 and 1970. Organized by topic, indexed and annotated, this is an efficient single-volume guide to references on many subjects. More sophisticated researchers will find this guide more valuable than Galin and Spielberg or Katz.

BASIC REFERENCE GUIDES TO SOCIAL SCIENCES & TO HISTORY

The basic reference guides listed here may lead the researcher to references in many subjects, such as wars, business cycles, and art history. These subjects transcend United States history, but references to these topics may well include citations relevant to American history. Therefore, these general guides are of value to researchers seeking the broadest possible coverage of a topic. Because of their scope, these guides include bibliographies which may be scarce and difficult to locate. If they are available, the bibliographies may be so specialized that they may include sources beyond the reach of the researcher for whom this book is intended. Such a warning is not meant to invalidate the usefulness of these guides. It is meant to put their usefulness in perspective.

The American Behavioral Scientist. *ABS Guide to Recent Publications in the Social and Behavioral Sciences.* New York: Author, 1965. 781 pp. Annual supplements. Organized by topic. Index. Annotated.

American Historical Association. *Guide to Historical Literature.* New York: Macmillan, 1961. 962 pp. This guide to the literature of the world's history considers more than the United States.

Besterman, Theodore. *A World Bibliography of Bibliographies and of Bibliographical Catalogues, Calendars, Abstracts, Digests, Indexes, and the Like.* 4th ed. 5 vols. Lausanne, Switz.: Societas Bibliographica, 1965-66. The listings of bibliographies in American history are in vol. 4, pp. 6,259-354. Organized by topic, indexed, annotated, this bibliography offers major general guides to American history found in other reference guides. It covers so broad a range of international literature that only a small part is relevant to persons seeking readily available bibliographies.

Bibliographic Index; a Cumulative Bibliography of Bibliographies. 1937-. New York: Wilson, 1937-. This index of bibliographies is *the essential tool* for research. Volumes, articles, essays, and lists in books are all cited in this most comprehensive general bibliographic index.

Boehm, Inge P., and Birkos, Alexander S. *Reference Works: History and Related Fields, with Research News on the Social Sciences and Humanities.* Santa Barbara, Calif.: ABC-Clio, 1967. 58 pp. Organized by topic. Index. Annotated.

Mason, John Brown. *Research Resources: Annotated Guide to the Social Sciences.* 2 vols. Santa Barbara, Calif.: ABC-Clio, 1968-71. Vol. I subtitled, *International Relations & Recent History Indexes, Abstracts, & Periodicals;*

Vol. II subtitled, *Official Publications: U.S. Government, United Nations International Organizations, and Statistical Sources.* Organized by topic, well indexed and fully annotated, this guide is a most valuable research tool. Almost any topic in the social sciences may be researched through leads discussed herein.

Stevens, Rolland E. *Reference Books in the Social Sciences and Humanities.* 2d ed. Champaign: University of Illinois Bookstore, 1968. 181 pp. A guide to the most popular and most commonly used reference books.

U.S. Library of Congress. *Library of Congress Catalog. Books: Subjects, a Cumulative List of Works Represented by Library of Congress Printed Cards, 1950-1954.* 24 vols. Ann Arbor, Mich.: Edwards, 1955. Supplements: 1955-59, 22 vols.; 1960-64, 25 vols.; and 1965-69, 42 vols. Available in quarterly and annual cumulations. This is a subject guide in volume form of the Library of Congress card catalog. Not every book held is listed here but the major ones are cited. Other Library of Congress catalogs are arranged by title and by author, but are of less value to a researcher seeking books on a special subject.

The Universal Reference System. *Political Science, Government & Public Policy Series.* 10 vols. Princeton: Princeton Research, 1967. Annual supplements. Organized by accession number. Excellent index. Annotated. See especially Vol. III: *Bibliography of Bibliographies in Political Science, Government, and Public Policy.* 927 pp. Includes references to many social sciences. Key word in context format may be difficult for students to comprehend.

White, Carl M., *et al. Sources of Information in the Social Sciences.* Totowa, N.J.: Bedminster, 1964. 498 pp. This guide includes essays describing the dimensions of various social sciences and the literature of each one.

Wynar, Lubomyr R. *Social Sciences General References.* 4 vols. Boulder: University of Colorado, 1963. See Vol. IV, *History; a Selective and Annotated Bibliographical Guide.* 347 pp. Organized by topic. Index. Annotated.

GENERAL REFERENCES TO AMERICAN HISTORY

The bibliographies included here are so broad that they cover the totality of American history, or are so general that they are not classifiable under categories in Part I of this *Guide.*

American Historical Association. *Writings on American History, 1902-1959.* Compilers, publishers, and coverage vary over the period. No volumes for 1904 to 1905 and 1941 to 1947. Cumulative index to 1902 to 1940 volumes. Yearly indexes. Not annotated. This list of all material published on

American history considers periodicals and books. It is the most complete bibliography in American history during its years of publication.

Beers, Henry Putney. *Bibliographies in American History: Guide to Materials for Research.* Rev. ed. New York: Wilson, 1942. 487 pp. Organized by topic. Index. Not annotated. This bibliography was the definitive one-volume collection as of its date of publication. Now in great need of supplement, it is still of some value. Students may find some references in this source irrelevant because they are typewritten, were privately printed and distributed, or are only locally available. Inclusion wrongfully infers they are available. Other bibliographies were too dated to be of value when included in 1942 and are now almost useless.

Handlin, Oscar, *et al. Harvard Guide to American History.* Cambridge, Mass.: Harvard University, 1954. 689 pp. Index. Not annotated. This guide is divided into several parts. General bibliographies and reference material are considered first, along with manuscript collections. The latter part of the book is devoted to topical bibliographies in chronological order.

Larned, Josephus Nelson. *The Literature of American History; a Bibliographical Guide.* (Reprint of 1902 ed. with suppl.) Columbus, Ohio: Long's Book Co., 1953. 596 and 37 pp. This old compilation offers excellent short comments about selected volumes. Well indexed, this work of over 4,000 titles is valuable for research in the historical literature through the nineteenth century.

Link, Arthur S. *Goldentree Bibliographies in American History.* New York: Appleton-Century-Crofts, 1969-. This is a series of 25 projected paperback bibliographies of special topics and all periods. Each has a different editor. Almost completely devoted to secondary sources. Author index. Minority of items annotated. This series compensates for inadequacies with broad coverage. Published bibliographies in this series are cited in this *Guide.*

U.S. Library of Congress. General Reference and Bibliography Division. *A Guide to the Study of the United States of America: Representative Books Reflecting the Development of American Life and Thought.* Washington, D.C.: G.P.O., 1960. 1,193 pp. Organized by topic and indexed, this guide includes only those books considered by the compilers to be the most outstanding books on American history. Excellent annotations.

BOOK CATALOGS TO SPECIAL LIBRARY COLLECTIONS

The catalogs listed below delineate the holdings of major special collections. Since these catalogs and supplements were published, new acquisitions have been added. Therefore, these sources should be further supplemented with U.S.

Library of Congress, *Library of Congress Catalog. Books: Subjects. . . .* Many holdings in these special collections are rare items or are unavailable elsewhere. Such references may be irrelevant to the researcher limited by time and research monies. However, these catalogs offer unique research leads and should be consulted. A nearby library may have important items in its collection.

American History

Author/Title Catalog of the Department Library, United States Department of Health, Education and Welfare. 20 vols. Boston: G.K. Hall, 1965. *Subject Catalog. . . .* 20 vols. Boston: G.K. Hall, 1965.

Dictionary Catalog of the Department Library, United States Department of the Interior. 37 vols. Boston: G.K. Hall, 1967. *Supplement.* 4 vols. 1968.

Dictionary Catalog of the History of the Americas Collection, The Research Libraries of the New York Public Library. 28 vols. Boston: G.K. Hall, 1961.

Anthropology

Author and Subject Catalogues of the Library of the Peabody Museum of Archaeology and Ethnology, Harvard University. 54 vols. Boston: G.K. Hall, 1963. *Supplement.* 12 vols. 1970.

Art

Library Catalog of the Metropolitan Museum of Art, New York. 25 vols. Boston: G.K. Hall, 1960. *Supplements:* 1962, 1965, 1968, 1971.

Blacks (Negroes, Afro-Americans)

Dictionary Catalog of the Schomburg Collection of Negro Literature and History, New York Public Library. 9 vols. Boston: G.K. Hall, 1962. *Supplement.* 2 vols. 1967.

Cartography, Maps

Index to Maps in Books and Periodicals, Map Department, American Geographical Society. 10 vols. Boston: G.K. Hall, 1968.

Demography

Population Index Bibliography Cumulated 1935-1968 by Authors and Geographical Areas, Princeton University. 8 vols. Boston: G.K. Hall, 1970.

Diplomacy & International Relations

Catalog of the Foreign Relations Library, The Council on Foreign Relations, Inc., New York. 9 vols. Boston: G.K. Hall, 1969.

Education

Dictionary Catalog of Teachers College Library, Columbia University. 36 vols. Boston: G.K. Hall, 1970.

Folklore

Catalog of Folklore and Folk Songs, John G. White Department, Cleveland Public Library. 2 vols. Boston: G.K. Hall, 1964.

Geography

Research Catalogue of the American Geographical Society, American Geographical Society Library. 15 vols. Boston: G.K. Hall, 1962.

Government & Politics

Subject Catalog of the Institute of Governmental Studies Library, University of California, Berkeley. 26 vols. Boston: G.K. Hall, 1970.

Indians

Biographical and Historical Index of American Indians and Persons Involved in Indian Affairs, United States Department of the Interior. 8 vols. Boston: G.K. Hall, 1966.

Dictionary Catalog of the Edward E. Ayer Collection of Americana and American Indians, Newberry Library, Chicago. 16 vols. Boston: G.K. Hall, 1961. *Supplement.* 3 vols. 1970.

Labor

Library Catalog of the New York State School of Industrial and Labor Relations, Cornell University. 12 vols. Boston: G.K. Hall, 1967. *Supplements:* 1967, 1968, 1969, 1970.

Law

Dictionary Catalog of the Columbia University Law Library, New York. 28 vols. Boston: G.K. Hall, 1968.

Navigation, Ocean Transportation, Sailing

Dictionary Catalog of the Library, The Mariners Museum, Newport News, Virginia. 9 vols. Boston: G.K. Hall, 1964.

Science & Technology

Author-Title Catalog, The John Crerar Library, Chicago. 35 vols. Boston: G.K. Hall, 1967. *Classified Subject Catalog, The John Crerar Library.* 42 vols. Boston: G.K. Hall, 1967. *Subject Index to the Classified Subject Catalog.* 1 vol. 1967.

Sports

A Dictionary Catalogue of the Library of Sports in the Racquet and Tennis Club, with Special Collections on Tennis, Lawn Tennis and Early American Sports, New York. 2 vols. Boston: G.K. Hall, 1971.

Western America

The Bancroft Library, University of California, Berkeley: Catalog of Printed Books. 22 vols. Boston: G.K. Hall, 1964. *Supplement.* 6 vols. 1969.

Catalog of the Yale Collection of Western Americana, Yale University. 4 vols. Boston: G.K. Hall, 1961.

Old Northwest (Upper Mississippi Valley): *Mereness Calendar,* University Library, University of Illinois (Urbana-Champaign). 12 vols. Boston: G.K. Hall, 1970.

World War I

Subject Catalog of the World War I Collection, The Research Libraries of the New York Public Library. 4 vols. Boston: G.K. Hall, 1961.

RETROSPECTIVE NATIONAL BIBLIOGRAPHIES

To 1800

Evans, Charles. *American Bibliography: a Chronological Directory of All Books, Pamphlets and Periodical Publications Printed in the United States . . . 1639 . . . 1820.* 14 vols. New York: Peter Smith, 1941. Reprint of original edition, 1903-34. Poorly organized. Index for each volume. Not annotated. The last bibliographic volume (XIII) considers 1799-1800. Vol. 14: *Index* by Roger Pattrell Bristol. Worcester, Mass.: American Antiquarian Society, 1959, is essential for efficient use of vols. 1 to 13. Supplement: New York Public Library. *Checklist of Additions to Evans' American Bibliography in the Rare Book Division of the New York Public Library.* New York: Author, 1960. *Checklist of Additions . . . :* organized in chronological order; index; not annotated.

Shipton, Clifford K., and Mooney, James D. *National Index of American Imprints through 1800; the Short-title Evans.* 2 vols. Worcester, Mass.: American Antiquarian Society, 1969. Organized alphabetically by author. No index. Not annotated. This is the comprehensive index for the American Antiquarian Society microform publication of every available title in *American Bibliography,* plus about 10,000 titles found subsequent to the publication of Evans' work.

1801-1819

Shaw, Ralph R., and Shoemaker, Richard H. *American Bibliography: a Preliminary Checklist [1801-1819].* 22 vols. New York: Scarecrow, 1958-65. See also: Shaw and Shoemaker. *Corrections/Author Index,* 1966.

1820-1871

There is no satisfactory national bibliography for these years. Roorbach, Orville Augustus. *Bibliotheca Americana, 1820-1861.* 4 vols. New York: Roorbach, 1852-61, omits many titles. Planned as the comprehensive bibliography for the years 1820-1861 is Shoemaker, Richard H. *A Checklist of American Imprints for 1820-.* New York: Scarecrow, 1964-. Meager in coverage and inaccurate, Kelley, James. *American Catalogue of Books . . . Published in the United States from Jan. 1861 to Jan. 1871.* 2 vols. New York: Wiley, 1866-71 is the only bibliography for this period. The only present supplement to the inadequate bibliographies of Roorbach and Kelley is Sabin, Joseph, *et al. Bibliotheca Americana: Dictionary of Books Relating to America from its Discovery to the Present Time.* 29 vols. New York: publ. varies, 1868-1936. The scope and comprehensiveness of this bibliography was constantly reduced as the goal of listing every book written about the western hemisphere increasingly transcended the editor's resources.

BOOK REVIEWERS

The usefulness of a book may be approximated without reading it. Reviews often serve as introductions and help the researcher to determine whether time and effort will be efficiently spent reading the volume under consideration. If the reviews indicate that a book will be useful, do not rely on the review for your information. Its opinions and conclusions reflect the attitudes of the reviewer. Use the book itself.

Book Review Digest, 1905-. This general digest covers only the most widely reviewed, and therefore the most popular books in the social sciences and history. Excerpts from reviews and criticisms are included. Arranged by author of book; subject index for greater usefulness.

Book Review Index, 1965-. Cites reviews of many more books than *Book Review Digest,* but contains no excerpts. Arranged by authors of books.

An Index to Book Reviews in the Humanities, 1960-. More specialized in subjects relevant to American history than other reviewers mentioned, this index also cites reviews without excerpts. Arranged by authors of books.

INDEXES & ABSTRACTS

Indexes and abstracts list periodical literature, books, and other published material which appear within the period covered by the issue. Usually these research services are published quarterly and are accumulated annually. These sources so comprehensively cover a subject that some topics may best be researched through them rather than through guides to historical literature. For example, a researcher may find more leads to information about the origin of the song "Yankee Doodle" in *Music Index* than in *Historical Abstracts* or *America: History and Life.* Abstracts differ from indexes in that they include brief (usually fifty- to two hundred-word) descriptions of the essential arguments or points of the writing described. Abstracts indicate better than do indexes whether publications are useful to research projects.

Guides to Indexes & Abstracts

Gray, Richard A. *Serial Bibliographies in the Humanities and Social Sciences.* Ann Arbor, Mich.: Pierian, 1969. 345 pp. This bibliography lists serial bibliographies, indexes, and abstracts by subject and suggests the most useful ones for a research project.

Kujoth, Jean Spealman. *Subject Guide to Periodical Indexes and Review Indexes.* Metuchen, N.J.: Scarecrow, 1969. 129 pp. A valuable guide, which briefly and in tabular form makes many of the same recommendations as does Gray.

Nineteenth Century Indexes

Frequently Used for Research in American History

Arranged chronologically by period covered.

Poole's Index to Periodic Literature, 1802-1906. This general index is not complete, surveying only a select group of periodicals.

Nineteenth Century Readers' Guide to Periodical Literature, 1890-1899, with Supplementary Indexing. 2 vols. Skimpy, but necessary as a supplement to *Poole's Index.*

General & Social Science Indexes of Twentieth Century Sources

Arranged alphabetically.

Annual Magazine Subject Index, 1907-1949. This index emphasizes sociology in addition to local and state history, omitting many scholarly periodicals covered by *International Index* (now known as *Social Science and Humanities Index*).

Essay and General Literature Index, 1900-. This is the only index which considers segments of books within its purview.

Index to Little Magazines, 1920-. Little magazines are usually short-lived and polemic in tone, but are often excellent sources of avant-garde opinion.

Public Affairs Information Service. *Bulletin,* 1914-. Frequently cited informally as *PAIS.* Public affairs is so broadly defined in this index that it includes many social sciences.

Reader's Guide to Periodical Literature, 1900-. This index includes magazines not considered by the scholarly indexes. Valuable for popular opinion and culture.

Social Science and Humanities Index (formerly *International Index: a Guide to Periodical Literature in the Social Sciences and Humanities*), 1916-. This index considers only the most prestigious scholarly journals of American history, but includes scholarly journals in all social sciences and humanities.

Subject Indexes & Abstracts

Arranged alphabetically by subject. Dates following titles indicate year coverage began, not year volume one was published.

Agriculture & Biology

Bibliography of Agriculture, 1942-.

Biological and Agriculture Index (formerly *Agriculture Index*), 1916-.

American History

America: History and Life, 1964-. This is the essential abstract of periodical literature in American history. Not only does *America* cover nearly all American historical journals, it surveys selected foreign periodicals.

Historical Abstracts, 1775-1945: Bibliography of World's Periodical Literature, 1955-. This abstract also is relevant to American history, with two important qualifications: only the postcolonial years were included, and only the most reputable journals were abstracted. This abstract stopped covering American history in 1964 with the commencement of *America.* The American Bibliographical Center plans to publish abstracts of articles on U.S. and Canadian history which appeared in *Historical Abstracts,* volumes 1 through 15, in a separate volume of *America: History and Life* (volume 0, 1972).

Writings on American History, 1902-1959. (See above GENERAL REFERENCES TO AMERICAN HISTORY.) This index is cited here although all historical literature, periodicals, and books are included in it. The majority of the entries in *Writings . . .* are from periodicals.

The diligent researcher will not consider his research complete on the periodical literature of 1941-47 and 1960-64 (the years when *Writings on American History* did not appear and *America: History and Life* had not yet commenced) until he has exploited two major historical journals. *The American Historical Review* and *The Mississippi Valley Historical Review* (since 1964 known as *The Journal of American History*) include a section at the rear of each number which lists recently published articles of all journals of American history. *Each issue* must be perused carefully, for there is no index to these lists. See also *Historical Abstracts; International Index,* and *Annual Magazine Subject Index* for journal articles of these years.

Arms Control & Disarmament

Peace Research Abstracts, 1964-.

Arms Control and Disarmament: A Quarterly Bibliography with Abstracts and Annotations, 1964-.

Art

Art Index, 1929-.

Biography

Biography Index, 1946-.

Blacks (Negroes, Afro-Americans)

Bibliographic Survey: The Negro in Print, 1965-.

Index to Periodical Articles By and About Negroes (formerly *Index to Selected Periodicals*), 1950-. Decennial cumulations 1950-1959 and 1960-1970.

Business

Industrial Arts Index, 1913-1957.

Business Periodicals Index, 1958-.

Catholics

Catholic Periodical Index, 1939-.

Crime

Crime and Delinquency Abstracts (formerly *International Bibliography on Crime and Delinquency)*, 1961-.

Demography

Population Index, 1933-. Also *Population Index Bibliography Cumulated 1935-1968 by Authors and Geographical Areas.* 8 vols. Boston: G.K. Hall, 1970.

Economics

Index of Economic Journals, 1886-.

Education

Education Index, 1929-.

Ethnic Groups

A Quarterly Bibliography on Cultural Differences, 1964-. (Although a periodically published bibliography, this research tool serves in a manner similar to an index.)

Geography

Geographical Abstracts, 1962-.

Indians

American Indian Index, 1953-.

Jews

Index to Jewish Periodicals, 1963-.

Labor

Index to Labor Articles, 1926-1953.

Index to Labor Union Periodicals, 1960-.

Law

Index to Legal Periodicals, 1908-.

Index to Periodical Articles Related to Law, 1957-.

Medicine

Quarterly Cumulative Index Medicus, 1879-1899, 1903-. Title varies.

Bibliography of the History of Medicine, 1965-.

Music

Music Index, 1949-.

Philosophy

Philosophic Abstracts, 1939-1953.

The Philosopher's Index, 1966-.

Political Science

International Bibliography of Political Science, 1952-.

International Political Science Abstracts, 1950-.

Psychology

Psychological Abstracts, 1925-.

Religion

Religious and Theological Abstracts, 1958-.

Index to Religious Periodical Literature, 1949-.

Sociology

Sociological Abstracts, 1951-.

International Bibliography of Sociology, 1952-.

NEWSPAPERS

Newspapers are valuable sources of information. However, because most of them are not available to researchers, special emphasis is placed here on the few printed indexes and commonly held microfilm reproductions.

Guides to Newspapers

Brayer, Herbert O. "Preliminary Guide to Indexed Newspapers in the United States, 1850-1900," *The Mississippi Valley Historical Review* XXXIII (September 1946): 237-58. This old article is the only source of information to such indexes. Used in conjunction with the following citation this article may make newspapers useful to the researcher.

U.S. Library of Congress. Union Catalog Division. *Newspapers on Microfilm.* 6th ed. Washington, D.C.: G.P.O., 1967. 487 pp. Organized alphabetically by community. No index. Not annotated.

Most Widely Used Indexes

Arranged alphabetically by title of newspaper or service.

Index to the Christian Science Monitor, 1960-.

The National Observer Index, 1969-.

Newsbank: Urban Affairs Library. Cumulative Index, 1970-. This service provides microform reproduction of articles from over 150 major United States newspapers, concerning twelve paramount social topics.

New York Daily Tribune Index, 1875-1906.

The New York Times Index, 1851-1908, 1913-.

Great Britain. *Palmer's Index to "The Times" [of London] Newspaper,* 1790-1905; see also *The Official Index to The Times [of London]*, 1906-. These indexes to this British newspaper are useful, for *The Times* frequently commented upon American activities.

Cappon, Lester J., and Duff, Stella F. *Virginia Gazette Index, 1736-1780.* 2 vols. Williamsburg, Va.: Institute of Early American History and Culture, 1950.

The Wall Street Journal. Index, 1958-.

DISSERTATIONS & MICROFORM

These two forms of research materials are of specialized usefulness. Library holdings in dissertations and microform vary so greatly that professional help is essential in order for a researcher to exploit these sources of information. To determine if a library has a copy of an unpublished dissertation, seek the aid of a librarian. The two most valuable guides to dissertations are:

Dissertation Abstracts: Abstracts of Dissertations and Monographs in Microform, 1952-. (Formerly *Microfilm Abstracts,* 1935-1951.)

Index to American Doctoral Dissertations, 1955/56-.

For microform reproduction of manuscripts, newspapers, rare books, and other materials essential to complete research see the following guides. However, the researcher should be aware that few of the materials in these guides will be available in any one library. For a list of the holdings by a specific library, obtain the aid of a librarian.

Diaz, Albert James. *Guide to Microforms in Print.* Washington, D.C.: Microcard Eds., 1961-. These annually published guides are the most comprehensive trade publications in this field. Useful for researchers is the supplementary *Subject Guide to Microforms in Print.* Washington, D.C.: Microcard Eds., 1962-.

Hale, Richard Walden. *Guide to Photocopied Historical Materials in the United States and Canada.* Ithaca, N.Y.: Cornell University, 1961. 241 pp. Although it is outdated, this guide still has value. If materials desired are not listed, they may be found in *Guide to Microforms in Print.*

U.S. Library of Congress. Photoduplication Service. *A Guide to the Microfilm Collection of Early State Records.* Washington, D.C.: G.P.O., 1950. Various pagings. *Supplement*, 1951. Various pagings. Organized by type of document. No index. Not annotated.

U.S. National Historical Publications Commission. *Catalog of Microfilm Publications.* 2d ed. Washington, D.C.: G.P.O., 1967. 21 pp. Organized alphabetically. No index. Annotated.

GUIDES TO GOVERNMENT DOCUMENTS & PUBLICATIONS

Federal and state government publications are difficult to exploit in research because they are published under nondescriptive titles, issued in small and limited editions, usually so bulky that libraries may not have available space, and are so varied that they are frequently kept in special locations apart from the major library collection. In order to use documents well, the researcher may wish to consult a guide which discusses the various types of government publications and how they may be used.

Body, Alexander C. *Annotated Bibliography of Bibliographies of Selected Government Publications.* Kalamazoo: Western Michigan University, 1967. 181 pp. Supplements, 1968, 115 pp.; 1970, 138 pp. Organized by topic. Index. Annotated.

Jackson, Ellen P. *Subject Guide to Major United States Government Publications.* Chicago: American Library Association, 1968. 175 pp. Organized by topic. Index. Annotated.

Leidy, William Philip. *A Popular Guide to Government Publications.* 3d ed. New York: Columbia University, 1968. 365 pp. Organized by topic. Index. Annotated.

Mason, John Brown. *Research Resources: Annotated Guide to the Social Sciences.* 2 vols. Santa Barbara, Calif.: ABC-Clio, 1968-71. Volume II is particularly valuable here, although some government bibliographies are also cited in volume I.

Schmekebier, Laurence Frederick, and Eastin, Roy B. *Government Publications and their Use.* 2d ed. Washington, D.C.: Brookings Institution, 1969. 502 pp. This is the most widely used and probably the most helpful single-volume guide to government publications.

U.S. Library of Congress. Serial Division. *Popular Names of U.S. Government Reports; a Catalog.* Rev. and enl. Washington, D.C.: G.P.O., 1970. 43 pp. Organized alphabetically. Index. Not annotated. This catalog is not the same type of source as the others in this section. However, it is of such great value that special attention is called to it here. Government reports are filed under their legal names, but appear in so many places under popular names that this catalog will save researchers seeking to use such official documents many hours of wasted effort.

TEXTBOOKS

Textbooks offer important leads for sources of information. In the suggested reading lists, authors usually cite books and periodical literature which offer detailed information concerning special topics. From these recommendations the researcher is usually led to studies of particular merit which are readable, persuasive, and/or definitive essays. In turn these studies will lead the researcher to primary sources. Some texts published since 1964 with valuable current lists of recommended sources are:

General Histories of the United States (All Are 2 Vols.)

Barck, Oscar Theodore, Jr., and Lefler, Hugh T. *History of the United States* (1968).

Carman, Harry J., *et al. History of the American People.* 3d ed. (1967).

Graebner, Norman A., *et al. History of the United States.* (1970).

Handlin, Oscar. *History of the United States.* (1967).

Hicks, John D., *et al. History of American Democracy.* 4th ed. (1970).

Morison, Samuel Eliot, *et al. Growth of the American Republic.* 6th ed. (1969).

Morris, Richard B., and Greenleaf, William. *U.S.A.: History of a Nation.* (1969).

Williams, T. Harry, *et al. History of the United States.* 3d ed. (1969).

Colonial America

Barck, Oscar Theodore, Jr., and Lefler, Hugh T. *Colonial America.* 2d ed. (1968).

Hawke, David. *Colonial Experience* (1966).

Economic History

Clough, Shepard P., and Marburg, Theodore. *Economic Basis of American Civilization.* Rev. ed. (1968).

Fite, Gilbert C., and Reese, Jim E. *Economic History of the United States.* 2d ed. (1965).

Kirkland, Edward C. *History of American Economic Life.* 4th ed. (1969).

Constitutional History

Kelly, Alfred H., and Harbison, Winfred A. *American Constitution.* 4th ed. (1970).

Diplomatic History

Bailey, Thomas A. *Diplomatic History of the American People.* 8th ed. (1969).

Bemis, Samuel F. *Diplomatic History of the United States.* 5th ed. (1965).

Ferrel, Robert H. *American Diplomacy.* Rev. ed. (1969).

Pratt, Julius W. *History of the United States Foreign Policy.* 2d ed. (1965).

West & Frontier History

Billington, Ray Allen. *Westward Expansion: History of the American Frontier.* 3d ed. (1967).

Clark, Thomas D. *Frontier America: The Story of the Westward Movement.* 2d ed. (1969).

Steckmesser, Kent Ladd. *Westward Movement: A Short History* (1969).

Southern History

Clark, Thomas D., and Kirwan, Albert D. *The South Since Appomattox: A Century of Regional Change* (1969).

Eaton, Clement. *History of the Old South.* 2d ed. (1966).

Black (Negro) History

Franklin, John Hope. *From Slavery to Freedom: A History of American Negroes.* 3d ed. (1969).

Civil War Period

Randall, James G., and Donald, David. *Civil War and Reconstruction.* 2d ed. (1969).

Twentieth Century

Barck, Oscar Theodore, Jr., and Blake, Nelson M. *Since 1900: A History of the United States in Our Times.* 4th ed. (1965).

Freidel, Frank. *America in the Twentieth Century.* 3d ed. (1970).

Link, Arthur S., and Catton, William B. *American Epoch: A History of the United States Since the 1890's.* 3d ed. (1967).

Shannon, David A. *Twentieth Century America* (1969).

Wish, Harvey. *Contemporary America.* 4th ed. (1966).

SERIES IN AMERICAN HISTORY

Many monographs, series of monographs, anthologies, and surveys include bibliographies of American history. The footnotes and bibliographies of these books offer important research leads. The studies mentioned below are noted particularly because they are most readily available to the researcher and are useful in developing working bibliographies in American history. There is always a variation in quality between the volumes of any series. Therefore, see book reviews for assessments of each title.

The American Heritage Series

Indianapolis, Ind.: Bobbs-Merrill. This series of primary source materials also includes valuable bibliographies and introductory comments. The bibliography in each volume is helpful. Arranged in chronological order of topics.

Peek, George A., Jr. *The Political Writings of John Adams* (1954).

Jacobson, David L. *The English Libertarian Heritage* (1965).

Heimert, Alan, and Miller, Perry. *The Great Awakening* (1967).

Morgan, Edmund S. *Puritan Political Thought* (1965).

Jensen, Merrill. *Tracts of the American Revolution, 1763-1776* (1967).

Levy, Leonard W. *Freedom of the Press from Zenger to Jefferson* (1966).

Kenyon, Cecilia. *The Antifederalists* (1966).

Ketcham, Ralph. *The Political Thought of Benjamin Franklin* (1965).

Adkins, Nelson F. *Common Sense and other Political Writings* [by Thomas Paine] (1953).

Friedrich, Carl J., and McCloskey, Robert G. *From the Declaration of Independence to the Constitution* (1954).

Solberg, Winton U. *The Federal Convention and the Formation of the Union of American States* (1958).

Gabriel, Ralph H. *Hamilton, Madison, and Jay on the Constitution* (1954).

McKee, Samuel, Jr., and Williams, J. Harvie. *Papers on Public Credit, Commerce, and Finance* [by Alexander Hamilton] (1957).

Dumbauld, Edward. *The Political Writings of Thomas Jefferson* (1955).

Ferguson, E. James. *Selected Writings of Albert Gallatin* (1967).

Roche, John P. *John Marshall: Opinions and other Writings* (1967).

Goodrich, Carter. *Government and the Economy: 1783-1861* (1967).

Peterson, Merrill D. *Democracy, Liberty, and Property: The State Constitutional Conventions of the 1820's* (1966).

Blau, Joseph L. *Social Theories of Jacksonian Democracy* (1954).

Post, C. Gordon. *Disquisition on Government and Selections from the Discourse* [by John C. Calhoun] (1953).

Thomas, Vincent. *Charles S. Pierce: Essays in the Philosophy of Science* (1957).

Bartlett, Irving H. *Unitarian Christianity and Other Essays* [by William Ellery Channing] (1957).

Graebner, Norman. *Manifest Destiny* (1968).

Pease, Jane, and Pease, William. *The Antislavery Argument* (1965).

Rose, Willie Lee. *Slavery in America* (1970).

Current, Richard. *The Political Thought of Abraham Lincoln* (1967).

Hyman, Harold. *The Radical Republicans and Reconstruction* (1967).

Clark, Thomas D. *The Modern South* (1969).

Filler, Louis. *Late Nineteenth-Century American Liberalism* (1962).

Quint, Howard H. *The Forging of American Socialism,* rev. ed. (1964).

Pollack, Norman. *The Populist Mind* (1967).

Ginger, Ray. *The Mind and Thought of William Jennings Bryan* (1967).

Lasch, Christopher. *The Social Thought of Jane Addams* (1965).

Resek, Carl. *The Progressives* (1967).

Commager, Henry Steele. *Lester Ward and the Welfare State* (1967).

Harbaugh, William H. *The Writings of Theodore Roosevelt* (1966).

Cronon, E. David. *The Political Thought of Woodrow Wilson* (1965).

Baritz, Loren. *The Culture of the Twenties* (1969).

Swados, Harvey. *The American Writer and the Great Depression* (1966).

Auerbach, Jerold. *American Labor: Twentieth Century* (1969).

Zinn, Howard. *New Deal Thought* (1966).

McGovern, George. *Agricultural Thought in the Twentieth Century* (1967).

Mendelson, Wallace. *The Supreme Court: Law Versus Discretion* (1967).

Broderick, Francis, and Meier, August. *Negro Protest Thought in the Twentieth Century* (1966).

Buckley, William F., Jr. *American Conservative Thought in the Twentieth Century* (1971).

Salvadori, Massimo. *The American Economic System* (1963).

Millis, Walter. *American Military Thought* (1966).

Cross, Robert. *The Church and the City* (1967).

Nelson, Harold L. *Freedom of the Press from Hamilton to the Warren Court* (1967).

Lynd, Staughton. *Nonviolence in America* (1966).

Ahlstrom, Sydney E. *Theology in America: Major Protestant Voices* (1967).

Abell, Aaron I. *American Catholic Thought on Social Questions* (1968).

Rischin, Moses. *Immigration and the American Tradition* (1970).

Bracey, John H., Jr., *et al. Black Nationalism in America* (1969).

American Problems Studies

New York: Holt, Rinehart and Winston. Approximately thirty volumes to date. Each volume is a collection of essays which present various interpretations of the topic under consideration. For the most recent list of booklets in this series see the publisher's book list available in most college or research libraries. This series is also cited in the most current edition of *Publisher's Trade List Annual,* New York: Bowker, under the name of the publisher.

Chicago History of American Civilization

Chicago: University of Chicago. Twenty-seven titles published in this series. Each volume is a brief discussion of a period or topic which summarizes attitudes of historians and suggests interpretations of the author. A bibliography at the end of each volume is helpful for researchers. Period volumes are arranged chronologically. Topical volumes are alphabetical by author.

Period

Peckham, Howard. *The Colonial Wars, 1689-1762* (1964).

Morgan, Edmund S. *The Birth of the Republic, 1763-1789* (1956).

Peckham, Howard. *The War for Independence: a Military History* (1958).

Cunliffe, Marcus. *The Nation Takes Shape, 1789-1837* (1959).

Coles, Harry L. *The War of 1812* (1965).

Singletary, Otis A. *The Mexican War* (1960).

Smith, Elbert B. *The Death of Slavery* (1967).

Roland, Charles P. *The Confederacy* (1960).

Franklin, John Hope. *Reconstruction after the Civil War* (1961).

Hays, Samuel P. *The Response to Industrialism; 1885-1914* (1957).

Leuchtenburg, William E. *The Perils of Prosperity: 1914-1932* (1958).

Perkins, Dexter. *The New Age of Franklin Roosevelt, 1932-1945* (1957).

Agar, Herbert. *The Price of Power: America Since 1945* (1957).

Topic

Bremner, Robert H. *American Philanthropy* (1960).

Condit, Carl W. *American Building; Materials and Techniques. . . .* (1968).

Dorson, Richard M. *American Folklore* (1959).

Ellis, John Tracy. *American Catholicism,* 2d ed., rev. (1969).

Glazer, Nathan. *American Judaism* (1957).

Hagan, William T. *American Indians* (1961).

Hudson, Winthrop S. *American Protestantism* (1961).

Jones, Maldwyn Allen. *American Immigration* (1960).

McCloskey, Robert G. *The American Supreme Court* (1960).

Pelling, Henry. *American Labor* (1960).

Rae, John B. *American Automobile* (1965).

Sablosky, Irving L. *American Music* (1969).

Stover, John F. *American Railroads* (1961).

Weisberger, Bernard A. *The American Newspaperman* (1961).

The Economic History of the United States

New York: Holt, Rinehart and Winston. This uncompleted series of eleven projected volumes has a well-deserved reputation. The bibliographies are eminently useful. Arranged chronologically.

Nettels, Curtis P. *The Emergence of a National Economy, 1775-1815* (1962).

Gates, Paul W. *The Farmer's Age: Agriculture, 1815-1860* (1960).

Taylor, George Rogers. *The Transportation Revolution, 1815-1860* (1951).

Shannon, Fred A. *The Farmer's Last Frontier: Agriculture, 1860-1897* (1945).

Kirkland, Edward C. *Industry Comes of Age: Business, Labor, and Public Policy, 1860-1897* (1961).

Faulkner, Harold U. *The Decline of Laissez Faire, 1897-1917* (1951).

Soule, George. *Prosperity Decade: From War to Depression, 1917-1929* (1947).

Mitchell, Broadus. *Depression Decade: From New Era through New Deal* (1947).

Histories of the American Frontier Series

New York: Holt, Rinehart and Winston. Nine volumes have appeared in this series on western development. Arranged in chronological order.

Billington, Ray Allen. *America's Frontier Heritage* (1966).

Bannon, J.F. *The Spanish Borderlands Frontier* (1970).

Eccles, W.J. *The Canadian Frontier, 1534-1760* (1969).

Leach, Douglas E. *The Northern Colonial Frontier, 1607-1763* (1966).

Sosin, Jack M. *The Revolutionary Frontier, 1763-1783* (1967).

Horsman, Reginald. *The Frontier in the Formative Years* (1970).

Paul, Rodman W. *Mining Frontiers of the Far West, 1848-1880* (1963).

Winther, Oscar O. *The Transportation Frontier: Trans-Mississippi, 1865-1890* (1964).

Fite, Gilbert C. *The Farmers' Frontier, 1865-1900* (1966).

A History of American Life

New York: Macmillan. Each of the thirteen volumes in this series is a major discussion of a topic in American history. Most of these volumes were written before Beers' *Bibliographies* was composed. Many newer studies have critiqued or expanded themes developed in this series. However, this was an outstanding series when published, and its bibliographies of primary sources still have value. Organized in chronological order of topics.

Priestly, Herbert I. *The Coming of the White Man: 1492-1848* (1955).

Wertenbaker, Thomas J. *The First Americans: 1607-1690* (1927).

Adams, James Truslow. *Provincial Society: 1690-1763* (1927).

Greene, Evarts B. *The Revolutionary Generation: 1763-1790* (1943).

Krout, John A., and Fox, Dixon Ryan. *The Completion of Independence: 1790-1830* (1944).

Fish, Carl R. *The Rise of the Common Man: 1830-1850* (1927).

Cole, Arthur. *The Irrepressible Conflict: 1850-1865* (1934).

Nevins, Allan. *The Emerging of Modern America: 1865-1898* (1927).

Tarbell, Ida M. *The Nationalizing of Business: 1878-1898* (1937).

Schlesinger, Arthur M. *The Rise of the City: 1878-1898* (1933).

Faulkner, Harold U. *The Quest for Social Justice: 1898-1914* (1931).

Slosson, Preston W. *The Great Crusade and After: 1914-1928* (1931).

Wecter, Dixon. *The Age of the Great Depression: 1929-1941* (1948).

A History of the South

Baton Rouge: Louisiana State University. The nine volumes in this projected ten-volume series contain some of the most influential studies of southern history. Some conclusions have been critiqued by later studies, but the bibliographies remain valuable. Arranged in chronological order.

Craven, Wesley Frank. *The Southern Colonies in the Seventeenth Century, 1607-1689* (1949).

Alden, John R. *The South in the Revolution, 1763-1789* (1957).

Abernathy, Thomas P. *The South in the New Nation, 1789-1819* (1961).

Sydnor, Charles S. *The Development of Southern Sectionalism, 1819-1848* (1948).

Craven, Avery O. *The Growth of Southern Nationalism, 1848-1861* (1953).

Coulter, E. Merton. *The Confederate States of America, 1861-1865* (1950).

Coulter, E. Merton. *The South During Reconstruction, 1865-1877* (1947).

Woodward, C. Vann. *Origins of the New South, 1877-1913* (1951).

Tindall, George B. *The Emergence of the New South, 1913-1945* (1967).

Localized History Series

New York: Teachers College, Columbia University. Each volume is a brief history of a limited geographic area or cultural group. Also included are brief bibliographies of topics considered in the text. Alphabetical by subject.

Pare, Madeline F. *Arizona* (1969).

Rolle, Andrew. *California* (1965).

Gibson, Arrell. *The Canadian River Valley* (1970).

Socolofsky, Homer E. *The Cimarron Valley* (1970).

Tucker, Louis L. *Cincinnati* (1969).

Ubbelohde, Carl. *Colorado* (1965).

Munroe, John A. *Delaware* (1965).

Kolehmainen, John I. *The Finns in America* (1968).

Bonner, James C. *Georgia* (1965).

Wittke, Carl. *The Germans in America* (1967).

Saloutos, Theodore. *The Greeks in America* (1967).

Judd, Gerrit P. *Hawaii* (1966).

Frantz, Joe B. *Houston* (1969).

Wells, Merle W. *Idaho* (1965).

Foster, Olive S. *Illinois* (1968).

Wittke, Carl. *The Irish in America* (1968).

Miller, Nyle H. *Kansas* (1965).

Clark, Thomas D. *Kentucky* (1965).

Rolle, Andrew. *Los Angeles* (1965).

Taylor, Joe Gray. *Louisiana* (1966).

Manakee, Harold. *Maryland* (1968).

Reid, William J. *Massachusetts* (1965).

McWilliams, Carey. *The Mexicans in America* (1968).

Fridley, Russell W. *Minnesota* (1966).

Moore, John H. *Mississippi* (1970).

Havighurst, Walter W. *The Upper Mississippi Valley* (1966).

Lord, Clifford L. *The Missouri Valley* (1967).

Brown, Margery H. *Montana* (1970).

Squires, James D. *New Hampshire* (1966).

McCormick, Richard P. *New Jersey* (1965).

Forrest, James Taylor. *New Mexico* (1971).

Rapp, Marvin. *New York* (1968).

Still, Bayard. *New York City* (1965).

Powell, William S. *North Carolina* (1965).

Haugen, Einar. *The Norwegians in America* (1967).

Weisenburger, Francis P. *Ohio* (1965).

Banta, R.E. *The Ohio Valley* (1967).

Gibson, A.M. *Oklahoma* (1965).

Stevens, S.K. *Pennsylvania* (1965).

Sanderlin, Walter. *The Potomac* (1970).

Powell, William S. *Raleigh-Durham-Chapel Hill* (1968).

Monahon, Clifford P. *Rhode Island* (1965).

McGowan, Joseph. *The Sacramento Valley* (1968).

Schell, Herbert. *South Dakota* (1970).

Alderson, William T. *Tennessee* (1965).

Cooley, Everett L. *Utah* (1968).

Platt, Doris H. *Wisconsin* (1965).

Derleth, August. *The Wisconsin Valley* (1969).

Homsher, Lola M. *Wyoming* (1966).

The New American Nation Series

New York: Harper and Row. This series of about forty projected volumes is the most generally authoritative and scholarly series of histories. Copious footnotes and extensive bibliographies are extremely valuable. Arranged in chronological order.

Gibson, Charles. *Spain in America* (1966).

Pomfret, John E., and Shumway, Floyd M. *Founding the American Colonies: 1583-1660* (1970).

Notestein, Wallace. *The English People on the Eve of Colonization: 1603-1630* (1954).

Wright, Louis B. *The Cultural Life of the American Colonies: 1607-1763* (1957).

Craven, Wesley Frank. *The Colonies in Transition: 1660-1713* (1968).

Gipson, Lawrence Henry. *The Coming of the Revolution: 1763-1775* (1954).

Alden, John R. *The American Revolution: 1775-1783* (1954).

Nye, Russel Blaine. *The Cultural Life of the New Nation: 1776-1830* (1960).

Miller, John C. *The Federalist Era: 1789-1800* (1960).

Smelser, Marshall. *The Democratic Republic: 1801-1815* (1968).

Dangerfield, George. *The Awakening of American Nationalism, 1815-1828* (1965).

Van Deusen, Glyndon G. *The Jacksonian Era: 1828-1848* (1959).

Philbrick, Francis S. *The Rise of the West: 1754-1830* (1965).

Billington, Ray Allen. *The Far Western Frontier: 1830-1860* (1956).

Eaton, Clement. *The Growth of Southern Civilization: 1790-1860* (1961).

Filler, Louis. *The Crusade Against Slavery: 1830-1860* (1960).

Garraty, John A. *The New Commonwealth: 1877-1890* (1968).

Beth, Loren P. *The Development of the American Constitution: 1877-1917* (1971).

Faulkner, Harold U. *Politics, Reform and Expansion: 1890-1900* (1959).

Mowry, George E. *The Era of Theodore Roosevelt and the Birth of Modern America: 1900-1912* (1958).

Link, Arthur S. *Woodrow Wilson and the Progressive Era: 1912-1917* (1954).

Murphy, Paul L. *The Constitution in Crisis Times, 1918-1969* (1972).

Hicks, John D. *Republican Ascendancy: 1921-1933* (1960).

Leuchtenburg, William E. *Franklin D. Roosevelt and the New Deal: 1932-1940* (1963).

Dulles, Foster Rhea. *America's Rise to World Power: 1898-1954* (1955).

Buchanan, A. Russell. *The United States and World War II*, 2 vols. (1964).

Presidential Chronology Series

Dobbs Ferry, N.Y.: Oceana Publications. Each volume contains a brief chronology of the subject's life, a few of his major statements, and a bibliography. For presidents on whom there is a full literature, the bibliographies here are superficial. However, for some obscure men, the bibliographies may be helpful. Arranged alphabetically by subject.

Bremner, Howard F. *John Adams, 1735-1826* (1967).

Sloan, Irving J. *James Buchanan, 1791-1868* (1968).

Vexler, Robert I. *Grover Cleveland, 1837-1908* (1968).

Vexler, Robert I. *Dwight D. Eisenhower, 1890-1969* (1970).

Moran, Philip R. *Ulysses S. Grant, 1822-1885* (1968).

Moran, Philip R. *Warren G. Harding, 1865-1923* (1970).

Sievers, Harry J. *Benjamin Harrison, 1833-1901* (1969).

Bishop, Arthur. *Rutherford B. Hayes, 1822-1893* (1969).

Shaw, Ronald E. *Andrew Jackson, 1767-1845* (1969).

Elliot, Ian. *James Madison, 1751-1836* (1969).

Elliot, Ian. *James Monroe, 1758-1831* (1969).

Sloan, Irving J. *Franklin Pierce, 1804-1869* (1968).

Farrell, John J. *James K. Polk, 1795-1849* (1970).

Black, Gilbert J. *Theodore Roosevelt, 1858-1919* (1969).

Furer, Howard B. *Harry S Truman, 1884-* (1970).

Sloan, Irving J. *Martin Van Buren, 1782-1862* (1969).

Bremner, Howard F. *George Washington, 1732-1799* (1967).

Vexler, Robert I. *Woodrow Wilson, 1856-1924* (1969).

Problems in American Civilization

Lexington, Mass.: D.C. Heath and Co. (Also known as "The Amherst Series.") Approximately eighty volumes to date. Each volume is a collection of essays which present various interpretations of the topic under consideration. For the most recent list of booklets in this series see the publisher's book list available in most college or research libraries. This series is also cited in the most current edition of *Publisher's Trade List Annual,* New York: Bowker, under the name of the publisher.

Reference Matter

HOW TO USE THE FINGERHUT GUIDE IN PREPARING TO WRITE A RESEARCH PAPER

The *Guide* is intended to assist you in gathering bibliographical materials—the literature relevant to your topic—from your library. The preparation of a subject bibliography is a time-wasting task unless you have a plan. A successful paper depends upon how well you have developed your subject from the sources available to you. You will ordinarily be required to find out all you can about the literature that relates to your topic. Consult your instructor, use the reading lists assigned for your courses, and read the bibliographies in your text and supplementary reading. After you have accomplished these first essential steps, use the *Guide* (and the worksheets provided) as aids in your library research.

Obviously, the *Guide*—in fact, all of your research sources—will be of limited use to you unless you have selected a viable topic for your paper. You will have the best results in writing a paper if you have done some general reading in the literature beforehand and if you are interested in your topic. Choose a topic that is within your capabilities; limit your subject in time and space. Do not, for example, attempt to write a "History of the Civil War" in a twenty-page paper. It is best to select a fragment of some historical epoch and deal with it in detail; and, as a general rule, it is advisable to work from the particular to the general. Do not attempt to perform research on topics beyond your abilities. If you know no statistics do not select a topic in which you must determine quantitatively normal and abnormal phenomena. In selecting your source materials, choose books and periodicals written in a language that you can read and understand (e.g., it is useless to add Tocqueville's original *De la Democratie en Amerique* to your bibliography unless you are literate in French—better to use one of the several English translations).

Before you venture into the library to use the card catalog or to browse in the stacks of books, you should spend some time in preparing a "road map." You can develop a fairly good idea of what you are looking for by preparing a worksheet (see the example on the following page). List the basic bibliographies from the *Guide* using the table of contents to find the appropriate topical listings. The annotations in the *Guide* will help in your selection. Use the card catalog in the library to find those works that are in the library, write the library call number in the space provided on the worksheet, and note in the *Guide* the reference number used to identify the work. You are now ready to locate the bibliographies you have selected in the stacks. Armed with a note pad and several sharp pencils, go to work.

Consult each of the bibliographies you have listed, and begin to make a list of the works cited in them that are relevant to your research. This is the point where your prior reading and preparation will pay off (i.e., be selective; do not try to make a complete list of books or periodicals until you have examined the few that seem most relevant). Use the page opposite your worksheet to list by author, title, edition, and publisher the titles you select. After completing your tentative list, go back to the card catalog and add the library call numbers. Before checking any of your selected titles out of the library, you should scan the table of contents, index, and appropriate textual passages to verify that each book is relevant to your work. It is good practice to make a few notes concerning the content of the books you intend to use in preparing an outline of your paper. Note that if the list of books available in your tentative bibliography is extensive (see the reverse of the sample worksheet), you may wish to revise the topic of your paper to further limit the amount of reading you will have to cover.

Prior to completing your bibliography, you should also refer to Part II of the *Guide* to select "General References" and indexes which will lead you to other rich sources. *America: History and Life* and *Writings in American History* are especially useful for short essays in books and journals. Note the partial selection of periodical articles taken from *America: History and Life* that are listed in the sample worksheet.

A term paper may (and a seminar paper should) be partially based on primary sources compiled by firsthand participants or observers of the historical event. Primary sources include diaries, memoirs, letters, the accounts of newspaper reporters, and court records. References to primary materials can be found in bibliographies and in footnotes to monographs and narratives. For example, to determine Franklin D. Roosevelt's attitudes toward Negroes, the researcher refers to the published papers of FDR and persons close to him. Books and articles on the New Deal and FDR will likely cite such primary sources as Samuel I. Rosenman, ed., *The Public Papers and Addresses of Franklin D. Roosevelt,* 13 vols., or Harold L. Ickes, *The Secret Diary of Harold L. Ickes,* 3 vols. Primary sources are the basic materials out of which a paper or report should be built. Secondary opinions of nonparticipants or nonobservers should be used to get to the primary ones.

Worksheet

1 Research topic: *What Were Church-State Relations in Early 17th Century New England?*

2 List topical bibliographies (from Part I).

Guide no.	Library no.	Author(s)	Title/Publisher/Year
529	BR51555	Burr, Nelson R.	A CRITICAL BIBLIOGRAPHY OF RELIGION IN AMERICAN LIFE. Princeton: Princeton U., 1961.
530	Z7757U5B8	Burr, Nelson R.	RELIGION IN AMERICAN LIFE. N.Y.: Appleton-Century-Crofts, 1971.
531	Z7757U5B3	Gaustad, Edwin Scott	American RELIGIOUS HISTORY. Washington D.C.: Service Center for Teachers of History, 1966.

3 List chronological bibliographies (from Part I).

Guide no.	Library no.	Author(s)	Title/Publisher/Year
566	Z1236G74	Green, Evarts Boutell, and Morris, Richard B.	A GUIDE TO THE PRINCIPAL SOURCES FOR EARLY AMERICAN HISTORY. N.Y.: Columbia U., 1953.
568	Z1236I5	Institute of Early American History and Culture	BOOKS ABOUT EARLY AMERICA: A SELECTION FOR NON-PROFESSIONAL READERS. Williamsburg, Va.: Institute of Early American History and Culture, 1965.
569	Z1237V38	Vaughn, Alden T.	THE AMERICAN COLONIES IN THE SEVENTEENTH CENTURY. N.Y.: Appleton-Century-Crofts, 1971.
570	Z1237W7	Wright, Louis B.	NEW INTERPRETATIONS OF AMERICAN COLONIAL HISTORY. N.Y.: Service Center for Teachers of History, 1963.

4 List general references (from Part II).

Library no.	Author(s)	Title/Publisher/Year
Ref. E1.A44	Eric H. Boehm, ed.	AMERICA: HISTORY AND LIFE. Santa Barbara: ABC-Clio.
		AMERICAN PROBLEMS STUDIES.
E195C7	Craven, Wesley Frank	THE COLONIES IN TRANSITION: 1660–1713. N.Y.: Harper + Row.
Z5305W6D3	Dargan, Marion	GUIDE TO AMERICAN BIOGRAPHY. Albuquerque: U. of New Mexico, 1949–52.
Ref. Z1236H3	Handlin, Oscar, et al.	HARVARD GUIDE TO AMERICAN HISTORY. Cambridge: Harvard U., 1954.
JA84U5M6	Morgan, Edmund S.	PURITAN POLITICAL THOUGHT. N.Y.: Bobbs-Merrill, 1966.
E191P64	Pomfret, John E. and Shumway, Floyd M.	FOUNDING THE AMERICAN COLONIES: 1583–1660. N.Y.: Harper + Row, 1971.
		PROBLEMS IN AMERICAN CIVILIZATION.
E161H5	Wertenbaker, Thomas J.	THE FIRST AMERICANS: 1607–1690. N.Y.: Quadrangle, 1971.
E162W69	Wright, Louis B.	THE CULTURAL LIFE OF THE AMERICAN COLONIES: 1607–1763. N.Y.: Harper + Row, 1957.

5 Visit the card catalog of your library to determine which of the references listed above are available. Record the call numbers in the space provided.

Topical Bibliography

[529] from A CRITICAL BIBLIOGRAPHY OF RELIGION IN AMERICAN LIFE:

F7F5	Fiske, John	THE BEGINNING OF NEW ENGLAND; OR THE PURITAN THEORY IN ITS RELATIONS TO CIVIL AND RELIGIOUS LIBERTY.	Delineates principle traits and its ideals; emphasizes the ethical impulses of the Puritan state.
BX9357M5	Miller, Perry	THE NEW ENGLAND MIND: THE SEVENTEENTH CENTURY. Cambridge, Mass.: Harvard U., 1953.	Features of Puritan intellectual outlook.
PS530M5	Miller, Perry, and Johnson, Thomas H., eds.	THE PURITANS. N.Y.: Harper + Row.	Relations between church and Society.
F67WH	Wertenbaker, T.J.	THE PURITAN OLIGARCHY. N.Y.: Schribner's, 1970.	Studies in history and characteristics of the "Bible State" in 1st half of 17th C.

[530] from RELIGION IN AMERICAN LIFE:

F82W5M6	Morgan, Edmund Sears	ROGER WILLIAMS: THE CHURCH AND STATE. N.Y.: Harcourt Brace Jovanovich, 1967.	Analysis of Williams' theory with its stress on moral law.
F7M63	Morison, Samuel Eliot	THE PURITAN PRONAUS: STUDIES IN THE INTELLECTUAL LIFE OF NEW ENGLAND IN THE SEVENTEENTH CENTURY. N.Y.: N.Y. U., 1956.	Studies in Puritanism as a transmitter of culture in America.
E169.1P41	Perry, Ralph Barton	PURITANISM AND DEMOCRACY. N.Y.: Vanguard, 1944.	
BR51657	Stokes, Anson Phelps	CHURCH AND STATE IN THE UNITED STATES. N.Y.: Harper + Row, 1964.	

Chronological Bibliography

[568] from BOOKS ABOUT EARLY AMERICA:

JK31R65	Rossiter, Clinton	SEEDTIME OF THE REPUBLIC: THE ORGAN OF THE AMERICAN TRADITION OF POLITICAL LIBERTY. N.Y.: Harcourt Brace Jovanovich, 1953.	Information on church-state in 17th C. New England.
BR52059	Sweet, William W.	RELIGION IN COLONIAL AMERICA. N.Y.: Cooper Square, 1942.	

[569] from THE AMERICAN COLONIES IN THE 17th CENTURY:

BR516G7	Greene, Evarts B.	RELIGION AND THE STATE: THE MAKING AND TESTING OF AN AMERICAN TRADITION. N.Y.: Cornell U., 1959.	In New England (17th) was duty of state to foster religion.
BR555C8G7	Greene, M. Louise	THE DEVELOPMENT OF RELIGIOUS LIBERTY IN CONNECTICUT. N.Y.: Da Capo Press, 1970.	Discuss Church-State relations in New England.

periodical Mead, Sidney E. "From Coercion to Persuasion: Another Look at the Rise of Religious Liberty and the Emergence of Denominationalism, 1607–1791." Church History, XXV (1956), 317–337.

periodical Miller, Perry "The Contribution of the Protestant Church to Religious Liberty in Colonial America." Church History, VI (1935), 57–66.

General References

from AMERICA HISTORY AND LIFE:

Hall, David D. "John Cotton's Letters to Samuel Skelton." William + Mary Q., 1965 22(3): 478–485.

Littel, Franklin H. "The Basis of Religious Liberty in American History." J. of Church + State, 1964 6(3): 314–332.

Stearns, Raymond Phineas, and Brawner, David Holmes "New England Church 'Relations' and Continuity in Early Congregational History." American Antiquarian Social Problems. 1965 75 (Part I): 13–45.

from AMERICAN PROBLEMS STUDIES:

F67H3 Hall, D., ed. PURITANISM IN SEVENTEENTH-CENTURY MASSACHUSETTS. N.Y.: Holt, Rinehart + Winston, 1968.

from GUIDE TO AMERICAN BIOGRAPHY:

F4A3 Adams, J.T. FOUNDING OF NEW ENGLAND. Boston: Little, Brown, 1927.

E19107 Osgood, H.L. AMERICAN COLONIES IN THE SEVENTEENTH CENTURY, vol. 1. N.Y.: Macmillan, 1904–07.

from HARVARD GUIDE TO AMERICAN HISTORY:

E289P4 Palfrey, John G. HISTORY OF NEW ENGLAND. N.Y.: A.M.S.

E376P7 Perry, R.B. PURITANISM AND DEMOCRACY. N.Y.: Vanguard, 1944.

Shipton, C.K. "Puritanism and Modern Democracy." New England Hist. Genealogy Register, CI (1947), 181.

Wolford, T.L. "Law and Liberties of 1648." Boston U. Law R., XXVIII (1948) 426.

from FOUNDING THE AMERICAN COLONIES: 1583–1660:

Mosse, George L. "Puritanism and Reason of State in Old and New England." William + Mary Q., IX (1952), 67–81.

from PROBLEMS IN AMERICAN CIVILIZATION:

F82W5G7 Greene, Theodore P. ROGER WILLIAMS AND THE MASSACHUSETTS MAGISTRATES. Boston: Heath, 1964.

BX9351W3 Waller, George M. PURITANS IN EARLY AMERICA. Boston: Heath, 1950.

Worksheet

1 Research topic:

2 List topical bibliographies (from Part I).

Guide no.	Library no.	Author(s)	Title/Publisher/Year

3 List chronological bibliographies (from Part I).

Guide no.	Library no.	Author(s)	Title/Publisher/Year

4 List general references (from Part II).

Library no.	Author(s)	Title/Publisher/Year

5 Visit the card catalog of your library to determine which of the references listed above are available. Record the call numbers in the space provided.

Worksheet

1 Research topic:

2 List topical bibliographies (from Part I).

Guide no. Library no. Author(s) Title/Publisher/Year

3 List chronological bibliographies (from Part I).

Guide no. Library no. Author(s) Title/Publisher/Year

4 List general references (from Part II).

Library no. Author(s) Title/Publisher/Year

5 Visit the card catalog of your library to determine which of the references listed above are available. Record the call numbers in the space provided.

Worksheet

1 Research topic:

2 List topical bibliographies (from Part I).

Guide no. Library no. Author(s) Title/Publisher/Year

3 List chronological bibliographies (from Part I).

Guide no. Library no. Author(s) Title/Publisher/Year

4 List general references (from Part II).

Library no. Author(s) Title/Publisher/Year

5 Visit the card catalog of your library to determine which of the references listed above are available. Record the call numbers in the space provided.

Worksheet

1 Research topic:

2 List topical bibliographies (from Part I).

Guide no. Library no. Author(s) Title/Publisher/Year

3 List chronological bibliographies (from Part I).

Guide no. Library no. Author(s) Title/Publisher/Year

4 List general references (from Part II).

Library no. Author(s) Title/Publisher/Year

5 Visit the card catalog of your library to determine which of the references listed above are available. Record the call numbers in the space provided.

Worksheet

1 Research topic:

2 List topical bibliographies (from Part I).

Guide no.	Library no.	Author(s)	Title/Publisher/Year

3 List chronological bibliographies (from Part I).

Guide no.	Library no.	Author(s)	Title/Publisher/Year

4 List general references (from Part II).

Library no.	Author(s)	Title/Publisher/Year

5 Visit the card catalog of your library to determine which of the references listed above are available. Record the call numbers in the space provided.

AUTHOR INDEX